full grown people

(THE OTHER AWKWARD AGE)

Greatest Hits

VOLUME ONE

Edited by Jennifer Niesslein

Full Grown People
Charlottesville 2014

Full Grown People
Charlottesville, Virginia
fullgrownpeople.com

First edition
Printed in the United States of America

Designed by Anne Hilton
Cover photo by Gina Easley

ISBN 978-0-9908301-0-8

To the Full Grown People community

Contents

7   **Introduction**
by Jennifer Niesslein

11   **Animal House**
by Jody Mace

17   **Autobiographies**
by Jill Talbot

27   **My Best Stupid Decision**
by Katy Read

35   **All Sorts of Things and Weather, Taken in Together**
By Randy Osborne

45   **Water from a Well**
by Sarah Pape

53   **Comma Momma**
by Kristin Kovacic

59   **Ashes**
by Jon Magidsohn

65   **Picking Up**
by Sonya Huber

72   **The Pull of the Moon**
by Meredith Fein Lichtenberg

82   **Getting Ginger**
by Michele Coppola

88   **Fear and Rafting on the Rio Grande**
by Zahie El Kouri

92   **Into the Woods**
by Rebecca Stetson Werner

103   **Lucky Girl**
by Jessica Handler

108   **A Gift for My Mother**
by Amber Stevens

116   **Fertilizer**
by Susan Rebecca White

121   Something from Nothing
by Carol Paik

129   Red-Handed: On Shoplifting and Infertility
by Jennifer Maher

136   Shelving My American Dream
by Dina Strasser

143   Fear
by William Bradley

152   The Pageant
by Shaun Stallings Anzaldua

157   Under the Bed and Dreaming at Hillside House
by Jennifer James

165   Proxy Sister
by Karrie Higgins

176   Hope Floating
by Robin Schoenthaler

181   Someone Stole Home
by Antonia Malchik

187   Eye of the Beholder
by Kim Kankiewicz

193   The Love of My Life, the Thief of My Sleep
by Sarah Werthan Buttenwieser

198   In Praise of Synthetic Vaginas
by Catherine Newman

202   Land of Shannon
by Suzanne Van Atten

213   The Return of the Dropout
by Sara Bir

220   Observations Brought Back from the Zoo
by Marcia Aldrich

225   Contributors

Introduction

By Jennifer Niesslein

The book you're about to read grew out of the Full Grown People website, which grew out of my own existential crisis. This is something of a professional pattern for me.

When I was in my late twenties, my friend Stephanie Wilkinson and I started a literary magazine about motherhood, in part, because I was freaked out about motherhood culture at the time. (These were the olden days, when magazines aimed at mothers were still the kingdom of professional nags.)

When I was in my thirties, I worried that I wasn't as happy as I might be. I wrote a book about it.

And the year I was to turn forty, Stephanie and I decided to shut down that literary magazine that had become part of my identity. I realized, after the fact, that I'd done something kind of stupid: I linked my personal life (the new motherhood crisis) to my professional life (the magazine about motherhood). By 2012, I was adrift. My kiddo was beyond the age where he needed me in the intensive way he had when he was younger, and I no longer had a job.

I wasn't alone. I looked around at my friends, and I saw that so many of them were going through some life-changing stuff. A couple of them were going back to school for new careers. A couple of others were either divorcing or getting into new romances. Plenty of them began shouldering responsibility for their own parents. Others, like my own sister, found themselves wondering what the hell to do now that the children were off on their own.

Perhaps like Chaka Khan before me, I'm every woman. In any case, I yearned for stories about how other people weathered this awkward age. And, boom: this is it.

*   *   *

Full Grown People is about transitional moments in adulthood. You might think that this is a coy way of saying "mid-life crisis," but it isn't. I don't ask the writers how old they are, but I know that some essays on the site have been penned by people twenty years younger than I am, others by people twenty years older, give or take. That's the thing about awkward ages—they can blow up on you at any time.

And yet. Sometime after the site launched, I was driving my teenage son somewhere—another awkward age, when the boy has so *many* commitments but no license—and I was listening to a story on the radio. It was about a woman named Pia Farrenkopf, who was found mummified in her Jeep, after dying some years before. No one suspected a thing until the bills that she'd been paying automatically ran her account dry. I'm paraphrasing the soothing voice of the commentator, but he said something like, "It was astounding to find out who she was. You'd think she was elderly, a recluse, but here Farrenkopf was, in the thick of life." She'd traveled the world; she'd created a career in finance; she was from a big family, although she was often out of the country. When she was found, it was the year she would have turned fifty.

"The thick of life" stuck with me. Because that's really what those decades between being truly young and truly old are, aren't they? They're not the thin broth of youth, waiting for ingredients; yet our lives aren't solidified, either. We're getting more acquainted with the hard stuff—the deaths, the limitations, the realizations that we can't make people be who we want them to be—but we also have the hope, the smarts, and the gumption to take what we've created of our lives so far and evolve.

*   *   *

This collection of essays is a sampling from the website from which it grew, fullgrownpeople.com. (You can sign up for updates at the site that come with little intros that I write.) There are way more gems on the site than I could fit in here, but I have to say that this anthology just straight-up delights me. The writers here bring all the stuff that gets my heart pounding: the funny, the smart, the poignant.

The topics here run the whole gamut: romance, family, health, career, dealing with aging loved ones, and more. But what draws everything together is the sense that we're all feeling our way along.

And we'll continue to feel our way along because, hey, that's life, right? No matter where we are, we're going to keep encountering stuff that we know, intellectually, others have dealt with already, but it still doesn't mitigate the feeling that we're winging it. "Oh, Jenny," my gram said when we talked last week, "how did I get to be *old*?" We laughed, but if I had my guess, I'd say the answer is just like this: one new befuddling, challenging, soul-stretching experience at a time.

Animal House

By Jody Mace

It's been a couple months since my dogs started wearing diapers.

So far just a few people know, mainly the people who have visited my house since the diaper regime began. I'm guilty of the worst kind of Facebook hypocrisy. When I post pictures of my dogs (and I do it a lot), I employ angles that hide their diapers. It's kind of like that studied angle that many women use for their selfies—the camera slightly elevated from the face so that the face is looking up. It's more flattering, but everyone knows what they're up to.

Before one friend came over, I texted her, "I should tell you, we're making both dogs wear diapers now. You will know soon enough."

I didn't want things to be awkward for her. There's not a polite way to ask about dogs wearing diapers and I feared that the silence would feel weighty.

My dogs aren't wearing diapers because they have a medical problem or because they're old. It's because they are acting like jerks.

My first dog, Shaggy, is an elegant little creature. He's a schnoodle, a schnauzer/poodle mix, and sometimes I think he's not really even a dog. He's got this meaningful way of looking into your eyes as he tries to speak English. He can say "hello" and "I love you." My husband, who is not as skilled at listening as I am, disputes this, but trust me.

Our second dog, Harlow, is not a specific breed exactly. He's a medium-sized, white hairy dog. Someone found him abandoned in a nature preserve and for reasons I don't understand, we took him in. He had clearly been neglected in every way for some time. His coat was a matted mess. He wouldn't take food from people. He didn't know how to walk up steps. He was distrustful of everyone.

We took him to the vet, got him his shots, and had him neutered. I took him to a behavioral trainer, one that looks beyond commands like "sit" and "stay," and, instead focuses on building his confidence and decision-making skills. I kept him by my side every waking hour, for months, at first on a leash, until he learned to follow me around, to come when I called. The change was like a miracle. He's relaxed now, and he bonded with us. He's got a sweet temperament. He's almost the perfect dog.

Except he pees everywhere. Everywhere. If we put a bag on the floor, he pees on it. He pees on the furniture, on the walls. Once my husband Stan was lying on a couch downstairs and Harlow parallel parked next to the railing in the upstairs hall and launched a perfectly aimed stream of urine onto Stan's head.

If I'm going to be totally honest—and at this point, what do I have to lose?—I'll mention that Harlow has also, on rare occasion, pooped in the house, too. It's a measure of how troublesome the urine is that I have no particular emotion when I find a pile of poop. It doesn't happen often and is fairly easily picked up. One time he left a pile that was perfectly formed into the word "HI." Since it was kind of a miracle, I took a picture of it before cleaning it up and posted it on Facebook. Then I learned that there are two kinds of people in the world: the kind who is disgusted by pictures of dog poop, no matter how literary, and the kind that suggests I create a line of greeting cards featuring messages spelled out in dog feces.

We had this idea, before we adopted Harlow, that it would be good for Shaggy to have a dog friend. That if he spent time with a dog and not just us humans, he would learn to be more dog-like. It turns out that he didn't learn much from Harlow. Except peeing. Our graceful, intelligent, little dog-person was now lifting his leg and peeing on the side of the couch. There really is such a thing as a pissing contest.

We worked more with the trainer. I don't want to relive it all here, but trust me when I say that we did all the things. All the things. Finally she dropped her voice and said, "You could try belly bands."

Belly bands are just what they sound like. Cloth bands that wrap around a male dog's middle, attaching with Velcro. When my kids were babies, I thought it was sort of weird the way some moms went nuts over cloth diapers and cloth diaper covers. I don't mean in a utilitarian way, but for the aesthetics. When I heard them gush about the cute patterns I thought it was a little pathetic. They're diapers! They're just going to be soaked in urine.

Now I get it. I started out utilitarian with the belly bands, buying just a plain white one for Harlow. But it made him look like an old man in tighty whities. Or like Walter White, cooking meth in the desert. So I bought a belly band with a cute peace sign pattern. And another one with stars. And one with tiger stripes. It made it all a little bit less sad.

I'm convinced that they have no idea why they're wearing diapers. They don't like them but they've come to accept them. When they come inside they wait in a little line for me to put the diapers back on them. If I could have just five minutes during which time they'd really understand English, I would tell them one thing: "Don't pee inside." That's it. I believe that if they really understood that I wanted them to never pee inside again, that they'd make their best effort to avoid doing so. They want to please me. And yet they do the very thing that pleases me the least.

Since we started the diaper regime, our life has gotten better. The dogs don't have to stay glued to my side. We're not cleaning the carpets all the time. Speaking of cleaning carpets, now I'd like to share with you the secret of getting dog urine out of carpets. This is a bonus, a takeaway from this essay, if you will. It's a process that's very inexpensive but time-consuming.

First you need to find the spots where the dogs have peed. If your carpet is tan like ours is, it may be hard to see the spots after they have dried. That's why you need a black light. Wait until nighttime, turn off all the lights, and walk around, shining a black light on the carpet. The urine spots will glow. Some other fluids will also make the carpet glow, but that's your own business and who am I to judge? Once you've found the spots, mark them by surrounding them with masking tape. Turn on your lights. Then spray a mixture that is 50/50 white vinegar and water. Soak those spots. Wait for them to dry. If you've saturated them sufficiently, this will take a day.

Next spray them with hydrogen peroxide that has just a little bit of dish liquid mixed in. Really lay this stuff to the stains.

When that's dry (and it will take overnight at least), sprinkle baking soda on and then vacuum it up. This gets out the odor and the black light test will verify that it did the trick.

So compared to that process, diapering a couple of dogs several times a days is not a big deal. Their diapers are almost always dry. The belly bands discourage them from peeing inside because there's no fun in it. So it could be worse.

But still, I can't help but consider the complexity we've added to our lives. Our kids, at sixteen and nineteen, are old enough to be pretty self-sufficient. I can forget to cook dinner and nobody is going to call child protective services. They can make their own damn macaroni and cheese. Things have gotten simpler for us from the days of busy, demanding toddlers who were hell-bent on electrocuting themselves and breaking all the eggs from the refrigerator. From those days, life has, year by year, gotten simpler. And yet, instead of taking advantage of the simplicity and lack of demands on our time, we did this thing that has made our lives infinitely more complicated.

We brought animals into our house. Sometimes when I think of it, the whole concept of pets seems bizarre. We do all these things to insulate ourselves from the unpredictability of nature and the outside world. We build houses, we seal the doors and windows. We avoid building a house on a flood plain. We install locks on the doors and a security system. We buy homeowners insurance in case there's an act of nature.

Then once we have this safe, controlled environment, we bring in animals. I believed all along that Shaggy was kind of a person. But people don't pee on the ottoman. They just don't. When the whole peeing thing started I'd sometimes look at these dogs and think "My god. They are animals." They seemed like just one step away from raccoons. Once I hired an expensive pest control expert to lure a raccoon family out of our attic. But we invite the dogs into our house. To live. We say, "Yes, you are a being who likes to chew on a beef bone that's been buried and left to rot in the ground for a week. But by all means please live in my house, which up until now, has been kept in a fairly sanitary condition. Here, sit up on the couch with me and I'll scratch behind your ears and possibly kiss the side of your face."

And they're unpredictable. When we adopted Harlow, we didn't consider the possibility that he would be an unrepentant urinator and that he would get Shaggy started too. But it would have been reasonable to assume that he'd do some things that would bring complexity into our lives. Dogs do all kinds of things. They run away. They bite. They bark at the nice couple pushing a stroller down the street as if their baby was the antichrist. They tear up cushions, leaving the cushion carcass surrounded by mountains of fluff.

I think about entropy a lot. I mean, I think about it on a superficial level, the way non-scientists do, because as soon as I start reading words like logarithm and microstate and quantum thermodynamics, I find that I need to quickly click on YouTube and watch a video of a chimpanzee riding a Segway. But the idea of entropy is that systems naturally move from order to disorder. If you put an ice cube into a cup of hot water, the water doesn't freeze; the ice cube melts. The molecules of the ice cube, which were frozen into a rigid order, are freed to move around as a liquid.

So is there also a sort of entropy at play in our personal relationships?

When things become too simple, do we have a tendency to add elements that complicate them? In a sense, any time we take on the responsibility of caring for another being, we're opening ourselves up to complications that we can't predict. How do we know that the child we bring into the world won't have a disability that will require us to reshuffle our lives? Or that the man we marry won't have a stroke a year later? We don't.

The issue of nurturing is all mixed up in this idea of personal entropy for me. I took in these dogs and that means I made a promise to take care of them, even if they brought chaos into my life.

I think we have pets because at a very fundamental level we have a need to nurture. And with that nurturing comes all kinds of risks. In the scheme of things, the diapers aren't a big deal. But every time I put a diaper onto a dog, I'm struck by the ridiculousness of the situation. Dogs, healthy dogs, wearing diapers. But I'm also sometimes reminded of the bond we share with these animals, and the promise we make when we teach them to love us. When Harlow learned to trust us, to sit by us and awkwardly lean against our bodies, looking at us as if to say "Is this how it's done? This love thing?" we lost the choice of letting him go. He was ours.

Autobiographies

By Jill Talbot

When I was in second grade, my teacher, Mrs. Croft, had us write an autobiography. She told us to add our address at the bottom, then roll it up, and tie it to a red balloon. That way, she said, someone might find it and write back. After lunch, we walked out to the large field by the school with our balloons in hand. At Mrs. Croft's count of three, we let them go. I can still see those red balloons floating up and away. I watched mine until I could no longer see it in the sky.

* * *

Thirty years later, I entered a rehabilitation facility outside Salt Lake City, Utah. We called it The Ridge. After a four-day medical detox that turned most of us into sleeping lumps beneath blankets in dark rooms, our first task was to write our autobiography detailing how we got there. The autobiographies were our way of coming clean, so to speak. They told us that if we didn't work through whatever instigated our addiction, we'd go right back to the bottle, the pipe, the pills. They called it "cognitive therapy": Read and Write Your Way to a Sober New You. To most of the people in The Ridge, a writing assignment was punishment, so it came with a privilege: to go outside. This was enough motivation for most, as the only chance we had to step outside was during the two thirty minute breaks we got between meetings that began every day at 7:15 a.m. and lasted until 9:00 p.m. And even then we were supervised.

I had been writing and publishing essays for years and even had a job at a university in the southern part of the state teaching students how to write them, but it wasn't until I went to The Ridge that I learned to stop hiding behind my own lies.

Since we were separated into groups by counselor, I didn't get to hear everyone's autobiographies, so in the evenings, I'd sit on one of the couches in the TV lounge and read the ones I'd missed. It was like being in a workshop, but one in which no one thought about the writing. The words were confessing. The words were admitting. And it made the writing immediate, raw, real. Years later, I'd teach an introductory course in the personal essay to a class of science majors who, until that class, didn't know the genre existed. Their writing reminded me of those rehab essays—the lack of self-consciousness, the art they had no idea they were creating.

*   *   *

No one in that place but me and one other guy had been to college. I don't count a college dean because she only lasted two days. Maybe she was too ashamed to stay. Maybe she couldn't do without her Vicodin. Most of the patients were railroad workers, farmers, or affluent, bored wives. Most had no job at all—the booze or the crystal meth made sure of that. The only patients who read on a regular basis were me and a twenty-two-year-old bartender.

The bartender woke up in the hospital and was told that he had passed out with a gun in his hand, a plan voided by a pint of vodka. Lanky, dark-hair, droopy brown eyes, now he'd be described as James Franco-esque, but then, he was the guy who liked to read. David Sedaris, Chuck Palahniuk, James Frey. He'd finish one, bring it down to my room. The small lounge across from the nurse's station had a bookcase, loosely filled with mostly self-help and Michael Crichton, John Grisham, and one surprising Joyce Carol Oates, so his girlfriend brought our requested copies twice a week: Cormac McCarthy, Richard Brautigan, Raymond Carver's *Where I'm Calling From*, because we both appreciated irony.

But we were there to write our own stories, detail every last drunk and destruction, the damages that had led us to the same exact spot, even on the same day, when we'd sat on a bench in early December, me drunk, him discharged from the hospital. That day, I'd stepped behind a glass door, then turned back once more in hopes that I could be let out, that it was all someone else's narrative. He'd been locked up behind a steel door after his shoelaces and the string inside the waistband had been confiscated. His drinking had come on fast, his reluctance toward his intellect its trigger, his final insistence on an artistic portrait of the disgruntled young man, a bottle of vodka, and a gun stolen from behind the bar. He'd woken up angry, embarrassed, feeling like he was living the life he had failed to end.

The last I heard, he went back to the bar for the afternoon shift, hoping, like some guy out of Hemingway story, that it wouldn't be as hard in the daylight.

*   *   *

One of the meth addicts had become so paranoid he moved into his workshop behind his house. He'd peek through the blinds, watching his wife and two teenage sons as they came and went from the grocery store, school. Then he had watched them move out.

*   *   *

My counselor's last words to me on the day I checked out: "You don't have to be Hemingway to be a writer. You don't have to be drunk or be sad."

*   *   *

They'd often tell us that the sobriety rate for people leaving rehab was ten percent, so that out of the thirty or so of us in there at any given time, three would stay sober. The rest of us would go back to drinking or drugs, or we would eventually develop some cross addiction. If we had been drinkers, we might turn to pills. Or pills might be replaced by cocaine. Cocaine by booze. It's a trick addicts play on themselves, they'd say, kicking a habit while forming a new one. They'd also warn that if we kept doing what we had been doing, we'd be dead. Some of us soon, because we had already done so much damage that "one more drink" would be too many.

What I had been doing was drinking Chardonnay, as early as ten in the morning on some days and as late as three in the morning some nights. I had loved a man for years who suddenly left me, who left our daughter, Indie, when she was four and a half months old. He abandoned us. But I abandoned us, too. I drank myself away from Indie, from myself, from the life she and I had together.

*   *   *

A blackjack dealer had worked downtown Las Vegas at the Four Queens during its opening years, her cans of Bud and a Camel as quick as the cards. The doctors said her liver was in pieces, shards, really.

Most of the time, she slept in her room, a vaporizer belching loudly beside her bed at all hours, her door propped open, the room dark even in the day, her frailty a shadow beneath intricate afghans and a green sleeping bag. She wasn't strong enough to walk, so we took turns bringing her meals on trays or holding her arm as she shuffled to the TV room. Once, someone found her on the smoking patio, her fingers fumbling to light a cigarette. Such futility, no more damage to be done. She was not well enough to attend sessions on schedule, and when she did, her head lolled to the side in sleep, her body bundled in that purple robe. She never wrote her autobiography. Either she couldn't remember it or it didn't matter anymore. When the coughs smothered her, we'd all look down at the floor or our notebooks, offering her the only form of privacy possible in a circle of people who saw her as a cautionary tale. At sixty, she looked eighty. Her raspiness, her weightlessness an ugly whisper from a fast life that not one of us envied.

She had been there at the beginning, she said, one of the invisibles shuffling blind under the blinks of the casino lights. "I kept a can of Bud right there at the table," she told me once. We regretted it for her, all of it.

The last I heard, her husband showed up, belligerent, demanding to know just how long she had been there before taking her home.

* * *

Being locked up in the rooms of a rehab facility for twenty-eight days, certain phrases got repeated until they were just noise, a skipping record: "Fake it 'til you make it." "It works if you work it." "Work as hard for your recovery as you did for your addiction." "You're only as sick as your secrets." The head counselor's favorite: "Don't sympathize. Empathize." He'd explain, at least once a day, that when people read their autobiographies or shared in a meeting, we were not to feel sorry for the person. We were to understand, to share the experience, to not distance ourselves with pity. The stories we heard were ours. Or they would be if we weren't careful.

* * *

A man checked out. He showed up two days later on the bench by the nurse's station. He had been badly beaten, or worse. Someone whispered about a liter of whiskey, a night in the ER, but we never got to ask him. They locked him up in the psych ward.

One guy who left The Ridge on the day I arrived hung himself a week later.

For my roommate, it took only two days before a bender ended with a mess of police cars in the front yard of her Park City home. Before The Ridge, she had done two stints at Betty Ford.

One man died within a month. Sober. He died from all the drinking he had already done.

One man disappeared.

I went back to the university where I had been teaching and made it to the end of the spring semester before I drove to the next town, got a hotel room, then spent the rest of the evening at the bar, convinced that if I didn't drink at home it didn't count. It wasn't a cross addiction; it was cross location. It was fucked up.

*　　*　　*

One of the railroad men had snorted coke on the long runs in the middle of the night. He chewed on plastic flossers during meetings and wore a University of Texas baseball cap backwards, even though he was fifty.

One night, I sat with him alone in the room where we usually played Scattergories. The room had one window, an elongated table, worn plastic chairs, a closet with extra blankets and plastic sheets. He was stuck at Step 1, the autobiography phase, staring for weeks at a blank page and a pen that would not take his disappointment, the guilt. So I sat across from him and asked questions about his ex-wife, the worst nights, their recent phone exchanges, and I wrote it all down. I asked until he had no more answers, so I started writing the questions then pushed the yellow legal pad across the table. I ducked out of the room, leaving him to stare at the vocabulary of his failings.

He claimed to be friends with a famous author, a woman who, according to him, had a framed picture of his chest x-ray prominently displayed in her living room next to a couple of hanging plants. He liked to draw spirals on the pages of my notebook during meetings. Once, during a session on dream analysis, he told about standing in the middle of a diving board. The psychiatrist on staff preferred Jung and told him that the board was an archetypal symbol of both risk and abandon. After we both left, we spoke on the phone once, me in my kitchen in Utah, he on his cell phone on a rail car somewhere across Oregon. The last I heard was his message on my voice mail: "I'm going to die here, but not before I see you first."

*   *   *

A train track ran adjacent to the hospital. I'd stand on that porch, watching the lights of the passing cars, and think about scaling the wall and hopping one. One night during a smoke break, one of the psychiatrists came out to the patio looking for me. He said he wanted to meet the Ph.D. who drank a gallon of wine every night. "You," he said, slapping my back, "are a legend." I said thank you, crushed out my cigarette, and walked back inside.

*   *   *

Every morning after breakfast, we'd line up at the nurses' station for our meds and blood pressure check. In the afternoon, we'd do it again. The girl who cut herself was on an antipsychotic drug. The hay farmer cussed and called everyone a "yahoo" before they took him off Prozac. After a weekend pass to visit her son at home, my roommate returned sedate and peaceful, nothing like the weeping, neurotic beauty she had been in the three weeks I knew her. Once when she was out of the room, I opened the top drawer of her nightstand and found three pill bottles and a cell phone. Contraband. I kept her secret and allowed the counselors to believe "she finally got it." One woman was on something that made her so drowsy she couldn't stay awake during meetings, which was a rule breaker. And the nineteen-year-old who had been sleeping in the backs of cars on the streets of Salt Lake City tried to charm the staff into giving him "something more." I stepped up to the window and looked down at the tray. The nurse held a white cup with two red capsules. I asked if I could stop taking them. She said she'd bring it up at the staff meeting. "Not a chance," my counselor told me.

*   *   *

"All of us," Montaigne wrote, "have within us the entire human condition." At The Ridge, they called them "autobiographies." Montaigne called them *essais*. In other words, attempts. Sit down and write how you got here. Try to figure it out.

* * *

I don't remember if any of the students in Mrs. Croft's 1977 second grade class ever received a letter from our balloon assignment. The balloons probably ended up popped or wilted, found by a stranger who had no idea that there had been words. Most likely in the panhandle of West Texas, they drifted into the middle of some field where the blades of a tractor shredded them. I kept all the pages I wrote from rehab. The fourteen pages of my autobiography, front and back, the notebook pages framed in spirals, and the pages from the Vietnam Vet.

He had worked the rail yards in Portland for seventeen years. He was heavyset, always in jeans and a shirt that struggled around his middle. When he sat down, he'd pull at it, this way and that, trying to get comfortable. He had gotten sober before and it stuck for thirteen years until he took some "stuff that blew his head off." He often fell into coughing fits during meetings and had to step outside for a drink of water, which was also against the rules. He'd shuffle back in, apologize, shake his head at his inability to get through an hour without breaking down. He had dropped out of school. Listening to him read was like watching a man dare the frail of a rope bridge.

On one of the last days he was there, he came to the door of the TV lounge and asked if I'd help him with something. We went out to the smoking porch where he pulled out a form and asked me to write down what he told me. He pointed to the four lines provided beneath the section: Addiction History. "Began using alcohol at the age of fifteen. Pot usage. Meth. Went to AA but stopped going to meetings. Thirteen years of sobriety. Relapse. Three years without alcohol. Came to The Ridge." I pushed the form across the table. He looked at the words as if they were details in a photograph he couldn't quite make out.

On his last day, he showed me to two chairs in the hallway outside his room. He said he wanted me to have something he had written. His counselor, also a Vietnam Vet, had given him a final writing assignment, one he didn't have to read aloud. He handed each one to me, in order, and while he sat with his arms folded and his head down, I sat in the chair next to them and read:

What Joe Lovett Like?
Joe Lovett was a yung idao spud. One hell of a grate guy that we called Spud. All he coughed is talk about Betty. He love to smoke pot and drink beer and stair at Bett pitchers. She was a pairty littal thing. He love to cut trees down with his fifty calorber gun. But we all now he didn't get to go home. He was the first of the three to be shot in the head. I will always remember him like a brother. God Bless him. He was bless of "19" of his life.

What Was Mike Stratton Like?
Mike Stratton was big boy. He look lik he cought cut trees down with two chops. But he was one big tedy bear. We all called he Miky. Miky was from Orchers Washington. He was ok until we got him riped. He cought of hurt any one of us when he was riped and in a rage. I got know Miky for only "26" days. He was number two of three to be shot in the head. In the short time I got to know him I loved him like he was my brother. Now I know whey we were num all the time we were there. We all tried not to think about it. Like Spud Miky was bless with "19 years of life. I will never for get them. They will always be in my hart and in my prairs. God Bless Them.

What Was John Bires Like?
John Bires was a nice guy. He wought have given you any thing. He was from New York. One of those guy that talk funny. He loved to smoke pot. Then he wought eat every thing. You think he talk funny. When he was riped he talked every funnier. I got know him longer than Spud or Miky. For fun we called him JB. Have you ever hered some one from New York called JB. JB loved to play cards. He won a lot of the time. I hated to play cards with him. He always took my money. I got to know JB longer than Spud or Miky. JB was there for two months. JB was three of three to die. JB also was shot in the head. But this time his head

landed in my lap. I just sat there with his head bleeding in my lap. I felt like I wasn't there. I will never foget them. I wil have them always in my hart. May God Bless them all my Brother.

*   *   *

It seems strange to feel inferior to someone's pain, to the levels of their addiction, but I always I felt as if I hadn't done near enough to be locked up with the others. I hadn't lost my daughter. Or my home. Or my job. I hadn't lived on the streets. Or gone to jail. I didn't even have a DUI, which seemed to be a prerequisite. Hearing such autobiographies made me feel one of two ways: Either I had no reason to drink, or I hadn't gone far enough with my drinking. I worried I was destined to return. Maybe it would take two years, or five, and I'd be back in the circle, reading a much more disturbing autobiography than Sunday morning Chardonnay.

*   *   *

Another thing: they always told us we wouldn't stay in touch. We didn't believe them. I didn't believe them. I was wrong. I have no idea where any of those people are—if they're sober, if they're alive.

Once we left The Ridge, we were like balloons released into the air.

My Best Stupid Decision

by Katy Read

The words surprised even me, tumbling from my mouth before my brain had a chance to process them.

"If you quit asking me for money for clothes for the whole school year then I'll, um … okay, next summer I'll take you to the European city of your choice, for a week."

"Are you serious?" my son said.

Wait—was I?

On that night last fall, my son wanted a new shirt. I wanted peace. Both of my sons, at seventeen and eighteen, have higher sartorial standards than my budget allows—just one of many catalysts for the wearying intergenerational conflict familiar to parents of teenagers. No doubt I could have gotten him to drop the subject for the moment. But drop it for a whole school year? In eighteen years of parenthood, I had not found a way to achieve that. Clearly, it would take a bribe. A big bribe. A bribe so huge it would cost about twenty times more than the price of a few wardrobe updates.

"Let me think about it," I backpedaled.

I thought about it, discussed it with others. Family and friends encouraged me, in the way of loved ones who like to imagine you having a delightful time overseas. My ex-husband had a different reaction, in the way of an ex who likes to imagine you paying your share of the college bills.

"*Oh. My. God*," he said.

*   *   *

Let me be more explicit about my financial situation, indelicate a task though that is, because this is the sort of story that certain internet types tend to dismiss as just another privileged person whining about her overblown problems. Fair enough, if your definition of privileged encompasses the middle class, including those of us who have slid down the ladder in recent years but are still clinging to a rung.

Yes, I know there are more harrowing recession narratives out there than "I stressed over whether to take the kids to Europe." But this isn't a tale of woe, really. It's a tale of recklessness, a tale of casting aside common sense, a tale of shelling out money to buy something intangible and possibly foolish, and hoping desperately that it was not.

For most of my life, I have occupied the reasonably comfy middle of the middle class. I have acquired—through a combination of effort, luck and, okay, privilege, not necessarily in that order—typical middle-class advantages and buffers: a college degree, job skills, a resume, some savings. These can be parlayed, at least theoretically, into moneymaking opportunities not available to those who lack them. I live in the city, in a neighborhood of tidy little houses and gardens, trendy cafes, lush parks that I go out of my way to drive past when commuting to work to remind myself how good I have it. By national standards, I'm doing okay, at least for now. By global standards, I'm positively swimming in luxury. The fact that I can physically scrape together the means to pay for a trip to Europe—while others lose homes or shoulder crushing medical bills or line up at dawn to collect their family's daily bucket of fresh water—unquestionably proves me fortunate.

It's just that I'm not quite fortunate enough to afford a trip to Europe.

The past few years have left me, along with many of my middle-class cohort, financially bruised. My ex-husband and I split up just as the recession hit. For the previous twelve years, I'd been a freelance writer and at-home mother, developing my writing career in exciting ways but never earning close to enough to live on. I had some savings, mostly invested in mutual funds and whatnot, which collapsed by about a third in the fall of 2008. Meanwhile, my former employer, the newspaper industry, was not only not hiring; it was shedding jobs as fast as it could.

I desperately needed a steady paycheck. And it appeared to be the worst possible time to look for one.

I sold pieces of writing here and there, mostly for sums that wouldn't have impressed a freelancer time-traveling from the 1970s. I slung sweaters at Macy's for a dollar above minimum wage. For a few dollars more, I worked shifts monitoring online newspaper comments and deleting the vilest ones. My combined paychecks approximately covered our grocery bill. Child support and a little spousal maintenance covered the mortgage and utilities. For everything else, I liquidated investments at recessionary lows. I was so scared to even look at my bills they sometimes piled up unopened—never a smart strategy for establishing financial health.

Finally, after three years of job-hunting, I got hired as a staff writer for my local newspaper. It's a fun, creative job and I'm thrilled to have it, but my financial problems aren't over. The job is part-time. Nearly half my income comes from child-support payments, which will be going away before long. My retirement savings are a fraction of what financial experts say you need —and that sum is more than twice what I will gross, at my current salary, over the next two decades. Retirement is a dot on the horizon, a distant posse in an old-fashioned Western, inexorably crossing Monument Valley as a silent cloud of dust kicked up by thundering hooves.

This was hardly the time to be jetting off around the globe.

Unless ... unless it was exactly the time.

My older son would be leaving in the fall for a college across the country. The younger would be a senior in high school. They would soon move past the stage of their lives—so endless while it's happening, so telescoped in retrospect—when taking a big trip with one's mom is a culturally approved option. They were almost grown men, and the image of a grown man traveling with his mother is considered so ridiculous that Seth Rogen and Barbra Streisand mined it for laughs in *The Guilt Trip*. Since long before Kerouac, young adults have hit the road with their peers. A young person's travel is a proclamation of maturity and independence, an act of mastering the challenges of adulthood, a quest with solidly mythological underpinnings—concepts squarely at odds, in other words, with our cultural views about attachments to one's mommy.

Said mommy, of course, holds a different perspective. Listen, I believe teenagers are programmed by evolution to drive their parents crazy—if they didn't, we'd never let them leave, and the human race would die out. My kids are admirably fit, in that Darwinian sense. But lately, the surges of annoyance had been accompanied by twinges of foreshadowed loss. Already, I was too aware of the sound my footsteps made in an empty house.

So as I mulled over Europe, certain stock phrases kept floating through my head. This would be the Trip of a Lifetime. It's good to Live in the Moment. I won't regret it On My Deathbed. Besides, Anything Could Happen: I might get hit by a bus or win the lottery (note to self: buy a ticket). And especially, What Is Money For?

Financial advisors would call these terrible arguments. I've written some personal-finance articles, so I've interviewed a bunch of them over the years. One time I made a bad joke about how I'd be living in my car someday. Politely but firmly, the financial advisor told me that's the way people talk when they haven't faced facts.

What is money for? Why, it's for security, these smart experts would counsel. It's to save for a rainy day, to replace a blown hot-water heater, to ensure a comfortable old age.

But what about the age I was right now? What about the ages that my sons were about to leave behind?

It's on, I told my son. We're going. And I offered the same deal to his brother.

*   *   *

I rented an apartment at a great price from generous friends-of-friends in Paris who were serendipitously leaving town for a week. First, we spent three days in Barcelona, thanks to a travel agent who explained that buying three nights in a hotel somewhere in Europe would cut the cost of our plane tickets, oddly, by more than the hotel would cost (if you glean nothing else from this essay, remember: always check hotel-airfare packages).

Barcelona was sunny and warm and relaxing. My older son practiced his impressive Spanish. My younger son rode his skateboard and took hundreds of pictures. In the afternoons, I left the boys to mingle with other teenagers on the beach while I wandered further down the sidewalk, past the huge glittering Frank Gehry fish, to a seaside café with wireless. I spent the afternoon of the solstice sitting beside the Mediterranean, reading and eating tapas (and posting on Facebook that I was spending the solstice on the Mediterranean, reading and eating tapas). In the evenings, the three of us ventured out for sightseeing and gazpacho, pan tumaca, paella, more tapas.

In a poetic way, I felt we were traveling back in time. When my sons were little and we spent most days together, I took them around to beaches and playgrounds and sliding hills and apple orchards. When they entered their teens and started hanging out with friends, those outings receded into the past. The boys hardly remember them now, and to them it's almost as if they'd never happened. But I remember them. And now we were enacting a brief, improbable echo of those long-ago adventures, with tapas filling in for Happy Meals.

Paris was cooler, cloudier, more contentious. It was June, but the air felt, at times, almost autumnal. I broke out my creaky high-school French. We saw Notre Dame, Château de Vincennes, the Louvre, Versailles. We browsed in a fashionable clothing store my older son somehow knew about. My younger son took hundreds more pictures. We climbed l'Arc de Triomphe's 284 steps. We ate escargots and cassoulet and pate and lamb confit and pastries. We sat up late around the kitchen table, discussing sights we'd seen and people we'd met, good-naturedly debating politics or culture, showing each other YouTube videos we liked.

We fought twice. The first time was mild. My older son complained of boredom after a couple of hours of aimless strolling around Île de la Cité. After seeing my feelings were hurt, he apologized. From that point on, both boys showed apparently genuine interest in every painting and statue and gargoyle.

The second fight was bitter. The boys were roughhousing in the garden at Versailles and I got angry. I was spending thousands of dollars on this trip, I scolded, and the least they could do was knock it off when I say so. The fight escalated through the evening until my older son swore not to speak to me for the remainder of the trip. Fine, I told him, I would leave his pre-purchased Louvre ticket on the table and he could do whatever the hell he wanted. He announced he would not be going to college after all because he could not stand to live his entire life with his mother constantly reminding him how much he owes her.

The next morning, as the boys slept in and I drank my coffee, I saw that he had a point.

My anger over the misbehavior was reasonable. But it stemmed, I realized, less from the money I was spending than from the emotions I had invested. I feared any conflict could mar our Trip of a Lifetime. Now here we were, in danger of ruining the whole thing.

So when he got up, I pretended the fight had never happened. My son followed suit. From then on, all was friendly and peaceful, or close enough. The fight didn't wreck the experience but became just another piece of it—another echo of what, frankly, things were often like when they were little and our days were punctuated with slammed doors and "you're the worst mom in the world"s, eventually followed, usually, by an olive branch from one side or the other: *"Clean slate?"*

*   *   *

A couple of years ago, I wrote an essay complaining about having had to sacrifice financial security in order to stay home with my sons. I criticized American cultural and workplace structures that tempt parents to reduce paid work to raise their children, but deny them a financial safety net, and even resist letting them back in the workforce afterward (a major contributor to poverty among older women). Some commenters and bloggers missed my point, thinking I regretted having spent the time with my sons ("Let's hope they never read this *and find out how much she hates them,*" one hissed). And more recently, other writers have begun publishing high-profile pieces expressing regrets at having opted out.

The fact is, I don't regret those at-home years. Especially not now, as my sons prepare to leave home. My neighborhood attracts a lot of young families, with its elementary and middle school, playground, and starter-size houses. When I'm out for a walk and pass little kids with their parents, I sometimes feel a stab of nostalgia. Then I remind myself that, though those years are behind me, I made the most of them while they were happening. However financially risky, that time was priceless.

Oh, I'd be much more financially comfortable if I had kept my full-time newspaper job all these years (although that's far from certain, given how many reporters I know who've lost theirs, including half the staff at the last place I worked). The idea of living in my car someday would just be a bad joke for a financial planner, not a sort of real, if remote—knock on my particleboard desk—possibility.

In my mind, I liken being a part-time stay-at-home mother to taking a long vacation I couldn't really afford. Not the relaxing kind, with umbrella drinks by the pool—more like an arduous trek through the jungle. But still, an expensive luxury.

Now here I was on a literal vacation, taking another ridiculous financial risk, for much the same reasons.

The analogy isn't perfect. I'm not blaming cultural pressures for my taking the trip, or asking society to make it more affordable. (Come to think of it, though, that would be awesome; I've saved receipts!)

The connection is that I did both things—two costly, possibly foolish things—ostensibly for the boys' sake but really more for my own.

Kids, as a group, are resilient and resourceful. I imagine my sons would have been fine in daycare. And someday, they'll probably manage to get to Europe on their own, if not too burdened with college debt.

But just as I wanted time with them when they were little, I wanted this last adventure, this last opportunity to just hang out, in a relaxed way, and do fun stuff together. What, in the end, is money for? In this case, it was for enriching my own personal Trip of a Lifetime. Not the eleven-day one to Europe, but the big one, the trip that takes you through childhood traumas and dumb mistakes and jobs that suck and ill-starred romances and unforeseeable crises ... and, when all goes well and you grab the opportunities as they come, some excellent experiences and wonderful memories.

*   *   *

On the plane home, we sat apart: the boys side by side, me a couple of rows behind them. I was absorbed in *Life of Pi* when my older son stood and twisted in his seat to get my attention. Look out your window, he gestured.

I opened the shade and almost gasped. Below the plane, the world was all white. It wasn't clouds. It was snow. Stretching to the horizon, for dozens if not hundreds of miles, nothing but blowing, vacant snow.

I put the movie on pause, unable to pull my gaze from the view. I squinted against the sunlight angling off that stark but dazzling land, a part of the world that I had never expected to see.

All Sorts of Things and Weather, Taken in Together

By Randy Osborne

My forearms and the backs of my hands are faintly speckled and sketched with blood. Like when, in grade school, you twiddled the ballpoint pen between your fingers and let the tip touch paper for quick, light slashes. Like when you made dots by pressing.

These traces on my flesh—they heal and are remade, but they will heal again—can pull a stranger's gaze, can make him look away. Neither defined enough to signify *cutter*, nor dug-out enough to say *crank sores*, the marks mean something else.

Squirrel.

*   *   *

Upon waking, *Sciurus carolinensis*, the Eastern gray tree squirrel abundant in my Atlanta neighborhood, yawns and stretches. It sees the world in color. Its hands bear vestigial "thumbs." Its body temperature ranges from 98 degrees Fahrenheit to 102.

Its brain weighs 0.25 to 0.35 ounces, relatively large for a mammal, in proportion to body weight. This is not because the squirrel is extra-smart, but because it has parallax vision (it looks at you with both eyes at the same time to judge your distance, for the purpose of fleeing) and spatial memory (it doesn't find buried acorns by odor alone—it *remembers*), and because a squirrel's keen sense of hearing needs more gray matter. Its ears face sideways, like ours.

The family name *Sciuridae* is Greek for "shadow of the tail." Used mainly for keeping warm and dry, the tail adds 17.8 percent of protective value to baseline when raised. Someone has measured this. Below the tail rests a cluster of blood vessels that the squirrel can dilate or narrow to warm up or cool off—no small matter for endotherms, creatures that make their own heat, like us.

You may detest squirrels. Many urban people do, given the raiding of bird feeders that goes on, given the chewing-up of attic insulation, which compromises our own heat-making, and given the mad, kamikaze severing of electrical wires. "Tree rats," you may call them, ignoring the many differences. I love one.

* * *

In June 2012, I was making more money than I had ever made. My first foray into the corporate world, with its murky, ever shifting demands meant a nicer apartment, with a pool and gym. My girl-friend Joyce and I dined at snazzy restaurants. We talked about having kids. My boss flew me out to work in the home office, a skyscraper that gleamed in the San Francisco sun.

Abruptly one afternoon, by phone, I lost my job. Downsized and restructured, I drifted, uncertain about my future. Ours. Although I didn't realize this when we met a few years earlier, the matter of children was a potential deal breaker, since Joyce half-wanted kids. "Not your willingness, I mean, but whether you would be open to the idea," she said, vaguely.

I was. With three grown kids from two previous marriages—three, by the way, is also the average size of an Eastern gray squirrel's litter—I felt ready to consider fatherhood with Joyce. But now I was jobless. Even before, there was a potential snag. Our ages differ by twenty years. The gap is wide enough to worry over, especially considering the already shorter lifespan for men. Twenty years is how long squirrels are estimated to live in captivity. In the wild, only about half that.

*   *   *

In August, a friend asked me to substitute as host of her literary reading series. A simple chore. Welcome the turnout, introduce each of three writers, and wind up the show, good night. But I felt nervous, an impostor. Although I had composed a few pieces that seemed okay, I was not a member of the scene, not a bona fide person of letters. I admired the others as they sped past, trailing bright streamers of irony.

Since I had planned to attend as a spectator anyway—and with, after all, not much else to do—I said yes.

We strolled in the near-dusk, making our way toward the coffee-house. I saw a few people I recognized, no doubt bound for the same place. Suddenly, someone cried out, pointing to a spot in the street beneath a massive oak. We hurried over.

A tiny curlicue twisted slowly on the asphalt, its sparse fur (*pelage*, I would learn) unruffled, eyes open. Blood seeped from the nose and mouth. Delicate whiskers (*vibrissae*) twitched. About twenty-five feet above us, we spied the leafy mass of nest (*drey*).

Joyce's artist friend Hilary retrieved an old tee-shirt from her car. She lifted the squirrel from the pavement as if handling smoke. Her fingertips arranged the fabric around its wee body, which all but disappeared. Most squirrels don't survive their first year, and this one fell hard. Internal injuries, most likely.

Of the night's event, I remember only the end, when Hilary approached me with the bundle, a cleaned-up nose peeking out. She had asked around—nobody wanted to take the squirrel home. Made sense to me, hardly a fan of the rodent class. Everyone probably recalled well, as I did, all the baby-bird failures of the past and couldn't face another. Hilary tucked the corners, a final tidying of the package.

"It's a boy," she said and held him out to me.

At home, after a Google search, I witnessed myself driving to Publix, where I asked the pharmacist for a batch, please, of one-cc, needle-free syringes. Then to the infant-care aisle, where I seized a liter of Pedialyte. Next, PetSmart for a can of Esbilac puppy-milk powder.

Removed from his burrito-style wrap, he fit in my palm like a miniature doughnut with a licorice-whip tail, or like an exotic, oversized insect. He kept his eyes closed, as if to say either, "Let me get some rest, it's been a long day," or, "I can't bear to watch what the human is about to do to me."

I loaded the syringe with Pedialyte. Here goes.

As soon as he felt contact, he gripped the nozzle with bony hands and sucked, eyes half open now, gulping, as my thumb delivered a slow push.

Baby squirrels in the wild gain sixteen-fold their weight in two months. In humans, this would be comparable to an eight-pound baby reaching 130 pounds in the same period. The squirrel mother's magic milk consists of twenty-five percent fat and nine percent protein. Compare Esbilac powder, stirred into Pedialyte: forty percent fat and thirty-three percent protein. Close enough, it turns out.

During those first weeks, Bug took six syringes of formula at each meal, with feeds about four hours apart. He would drain the first syringe, swat it away, and grope frantically for the next. In about a month, he was downing less formula and rejecting the syringe after emptying two or three. He munched bits of apple. A few weeks later, diced raw green beans, and broccoli stems. Shelled nuts. Before long, he was cracking into them himself.

*   *   *

"Imagine," the wildlife rehabber tells me, "having a two-year-old child who is emotionally dependent on you—only you, they latch onto a single caregiver—and who will never grow up. I mean never."

I think of my kids as two-year-olds. Hadn't I wanted them to grow up? Of course, I did. Yes. And: no.

The rehabber is realistic in describing my options. She is predicting from experience how things will go. Did she say "emotionally"?

Until her, I didn't know that people exist who specialize in the process of returning squirrels to their natural habitat, after well-meaning humans like me snatch them out.

"But it doesn't always work," she says.

I keep her number.

*   *   *

"The majority of mammals live solitary lives; estimates suggest that at least 85 percent of mammals can be classified as asocial animals that aggregate only briefly at a seasonal food source or to mate."

—Michael Steele and John Kropowski, *North American Tree Squirrels* (Smithsonian Books, 2001)

Joyce and I watch squirrels jump, dart, and scurry in the park. On a flat surface, squirrels can travel as fast as 16.7 miles per hour. Their crazy trajectories, never in tandem or together, bisect each other across the grass and up the trunks of trees. Lyrics from a Patti Smith song come to me, the one she wrote for Robert Mapplethorpe as he was dying of AIDS. "Paths that cross will cross again."

In the traffic behind us on North Highland Avenue, we hear a pop—the sound a plastic bag with trapped air makes as tires roll over it.

Together, we turn. The squirrel lies near the center of the road, still alive, hands clawing pavement, unable to drag the rest of its body. After a few seconds, stillness. A light, almost merry wave of the tail, goodbye.

How far away the curb must have seemed, in that squirrel's fast-fading, parallax, big-brained vision. The Stephen Dobyns poem, "Querencia" (Spanish for "a secure place"), describes a bull tormented in the ring as the audience cheers.

Probably, he has no real knowledge and,
like any of us, it's pain that teaches him
to be wary, so his only desire in defeat
is to return to that spot of sand, and even
when dying he will stagger toward his querencia
as if he might feel better there, could

recover there, take back his strength, win
the fight, stick that glittering creature to the wall ...

The glittering creature in this instance is not a matador but an SUV, now a block away. No bloodthirsty crowd, only a few pedestrians who seem not to notice what happened. Maybe the driver didn't, either.

One of the many reliefs of no longer owning a car is that I don't have to worry about killing anything with it, but I remember instances. A thump, the glance in the rear-view mirror. That wad of flopping misery. My sick, jarred sense of a fatal suffering so great and so nearby, yet unfelt by me, impossibly, its cause.

In Dobyns's poem, the afternoon proceeds messily, the bullfighter proves inept, and "everyone wanted to forget it and go home." Joyce and I do, too. Cars make sad arcs around the squirrel corpse, which I know I should relocate before it's transformed into a meat rag.

The squirrel's up-tilted, almond-shaped eye, with that tight rim of lighter hair, is still moist and shiny. I've had my eye inches from Bug's. Like this eye, his are strong-coffee opaque, yet suggestive of a depth.

The body is warm in my hands. I think of Hilary's fingers. I feel crushed bone pieces, many bone pieces, jostle amid the limp flesh. Before situating it in the grass, I sneak a glimpse at the lower abdomen, the pink nub there. Male.

*   *   *

Tonight's sunset must be glorious to somebody. On Elizabeth Street, I stand gaping, unfazed, at the orange-scarlet and indigo riot in the sky.

I'm hungry.

Scientists at Wake Forest University devised a chamber with an oxygen analyzer, put a squirrel inside, and gave it something to eat. The idea was to find out whether squirrels know which nuts are smartest to consume, i.e., which offer a "net value" (calories) that justifies their "handling costs" (effort taken to split the shell, determined by oxygen use). As you may have guessed, they do know. They budget every sliver of energy. Gray squirrels do not hibernate, which means that, even in the harshest winter, they forage. Searching and often not finding.

Squirrels budget, and so must we, the privileged. Dinner done— burritos, cheap New Zealand white wine—it's playtime for Bug. He's ready. He charges madly up and down the levels of his tall cage. We do this twice a day, to keep his skeleton supple and because I can't resist him.

Metabolic bone disease is the main cause of death in captive squirrels. Like humans, when they are not exposed to enough sunlight, they make no vitamin D and can't absorb calcium. I send away for Bug's food. The fortified blocks, in sealed plastic bags from Florida, consist of pecans, protein isolates (whey, wheat), and thirty other ingredients, including vitamins D, K, E, as well as B-1, -2, -3, -6, and -12, with all the important minerals. A month's supply, twenty-five dollars.

He springs out. Perches on my shoulder, rotates to inspect the room. Hops atop my head.

For the next hour, he scrambles over and across my arms, legs, hands, and torso—somehow he knows to avoid my face—pausing only to wrestle. This involves tumbling between my hands, losing then regaining the top position. Over and over.

He nips, and I feel the promise of his incisors, but not their full gift. The damage is done by his inward-curved claws. Evolved for tree bark, they slice and puncture flesh. I endure this abuse in trade for the moments between, when I touch his pelage, soft belly, and cold wet nose. His tail, plumy, snow-fringed, sifts through my fingers.

I offer a hazelnut, which he snatches and "buries"—finds a cranny in the sofa or an empty shoe or even a vacant pocket, jams the nut in as far as possible, and pats around the area. *Scatterhoarding.* During play, he will not stop longer than a few seconds.

In the mornings, though—yawn and stretch—he positions himself on the cage's upper tier, where I can reach him, tucks his snout into the crook of my thumb, and submits to a few minutes of drowsy massage. As if he knows breakfast follows. He does know.

*   *   *

One of Emerson's lesser-known poems, "Fable," pits squirrel against mountain in an argument—the dialogue of big versus small, hashing out superiority. Says the squirrel,

But all sorts of things and weather
Must be taken in together
To make up a year
And a sphere.
And I think it's no disgrace
To occupy my place.

It reminds me of Bergson's *Introduction to Metaphysics*, where he writes that "many diverse images, borrowed from very different orders of things, may, by the convergence of their action, direct consciousness to the precise point where there is a certain intuition to be seized." But toward what is Bug directing me? What am I expected to seize?

*   *   *

Squirrels mate twice per year, once between December and February, and again in summer. Estrus lasts eight hours. All day, males chase the female, who copulates with three or four. Each gets about twenty seconds. The older, dominant ones usually prevail, but not always. In "breakaways," the female escapes to a secluded area for a few minutes of peace. She mates with the first male that finds her.

Bug's downy testicles are huge, about the size of butterbeans, loaded with baby-making potential. In "active" mode, his balls weigh seven grams. They shrink to one gram when the season of lust passes. Why shouldn't he get his chance? Even if it's with a girl who's just tired of going through the paces with more virile types and willing to take whatever guy comes along.

But I fear for him in the wild. Predators hover and lurk. Hawks and owls. Cats, foxes, and snakes. The hodgepodge of parasitic species that want him includes six protozoans, two flukes, 10 tapeworms, one acanthocephalan (thorny-headed worm), 23 roundworms, 37 mites, seven lice, and 17 fleas. There is also the odious botfly, which lays its eggs under the squirrel's skin. Larvae become disfiguring lumps the size of olives, called "warbles." Eventually, the pupa drop out of dermal holes to finish growing in soil.

What's mating worth?

* * *

In the fall of 2013, I see reports of squirrel migrations in north Georgia. A bumper crop of oak acorns in the previous year led to a high birth rate, followed by a mild winter and rainy spring, which caused the supply of nuts from oak, beech, and hickory trees (mast) to dwindle. That's one theory. Less obvious forces could be responsible. Naturalist P.R. Hoy of Racine, Wisconsin, reported gray squirrel migrations across his territory during three satisfactory mast years—1842 (four weeks, a half-billion squirrels!), 1847, and 1852. No one knows why.

In more recent history, our state has not seen a migration of 2013's magnitude since 1968, a year when other stories pushed aside news of wandering *Sciuridae*. The war in Vietnam raged that year, with the Tet offensive in January and the My Lai massacre in March. Martin Luther King, Jr., was killed in April and Robert F. Kennedy in June. President Lyndon Johnson gave up on seeking a second term.

Quieter history was made in Greenwich Village. "In retrospect, the summer of 1968 marked a time of physical awakening for both Robert and me," writes Patti Smith in her memoir. They had begun to understand what was possible, and what was not.

* * *

Winter's almost here. Joyce and I continue our talks. I bring up parenthood more often than she does, she who has yet to become a mother (*nulliparous*). At the same time, I wonder about my fitness for doing the dad thing yet again.

For more than a year Bug was, other than Joyce, the last thing I saw before sleep, and the first thing I saw in the morning, his cage and towel "nest" situated opposite our bed. I woke to the squeaks when he dreamed.

At odd moments, almost every day, memories of him rise. Images. Sniffing inside my ear. Smacking on a chunk of avocado, his favorite. Balancing on my hand, his teeth scraping my thumbnail. Nuzzling me as, from the other side of the bars, I trace his flanks and ribs. I feel his heart tapping.

I see him leap from branch to branch in the forest canopy, his body made for this. The "overstory," botanists call the green ceiling, limbs almost entwined, leaf and twig so close together that the vibrissae of tree squirrels grow longer than those of ground squirrels, the better to detect what's near. There's an "understory," too, down where I am. Paths that cross will cross again. I picture him in mid-air.

———
———

Water from a Well

By Sarah Pape

Roger lived in the kind of house I coveted: a swatch of deep
green manicured lawn, the clean white paint of a new development, and high ceilings. The higher the ceilings, the more desirable
the home. That's what I thought at nineteen, living in a two-bedroom
apartment where, when you flipped on the light, cockroaches scattered. This was our first place as a family—Rik, me, and our seven-
month-old baby, Sylvia. We'd just gotten married and everything we
owned was second hand. We would go to yard sales every weekend,
holding things up to each other, as if to say, "This? Is this what grown
ups own?"

We bought a little tabletop ironing board and an iron so that I could
press Rik's thrift store button-ups and slacks. He was working at a
dealership trying his best to sell cars to people who wandered onto
the lot. He didn't have the bloodlust for it and would come home
dejected and wrinkled after sweating all day on the blacktop. We were
living off of meager commissions and mercy checks from my family,
waking up every morning with the dread of having to make another
call—either to the bank to argue overdraft charges or to feign a casual
tone as I worked up the courage to call my mom or grandparents to

ask for more.

Late one night, I picked up the worn Want Ads that Rik had fallen asleep with and began looking for something I could do. I only had one year of community college under my belt, but I could type and write. I began feeding a fantasy of becoming a secret shopper or someone who "makes money from home," going so far as to pay fifty dollars to get the catalogue for products one could assemble. It turned out to be dollhouse furniture. They would send you the pieces. I did the math and realized it would take thousands of tiny desks and bunk beds to even pay the electricity bill.

Then I saw Roger's ad in the Personal Services section: "I'm a disabled man in need of light cleaning, grocery shopping, and assistance with physical exercise. Some experience necessary." We had only lived on our own for a few months, but I was learning quickly how to manage the domestic. I wasn't meticulous, but we cleaned enough to hold the roaches back. I knew how to shop on a budget. In fact, some nights I would take the baby and go wander the aisles of a store, loading up the cart and then putting everything back. I was rehearsing for the day that we would have enough money and could buy whatever we wanted. That's what success meant to me then. That's why I was practically salivating when I pulled up to the white tract house when I arrived for an interview the next day.

*   *   *

People in wheelchairs don't scare me. My grandmother, who had contracted polio at twenty-five, lived her life—and mine—on wheels. My cousin and I would fight over her chair when she would get into her recliner for an afternoon nap, using a slide board to bridge the distance between the wheelchair and her destination. Careening down the long, marble hallways, we could balance on the back wheels, spinning in circles. As we got older, Nonie needed more help getting in and out of her chair. They eventually bought a nylon sling that hooked to a manual lift. Once you hooked each corner to the mechanism, you pumped a lever that incrementally lifted her into the air. She would hang there in the cradle of the nylon sling as you wheeled her to where she wanted to go.

It was my experience with this that convinced Roger to hire me. He was impressed that I knew what a Hoyer Lift was and that I could easily identify all of its parts. That first day, he showed me around his huge three-bedroom house: the office where he had a massive computer set-up with voice recognition, his kitchen with flats of Gatorade and Mountain Dew, his bedroom with one wall covered from floor to ceiling with jerseys and t-shirts signed by rock stars and athletes. He loved heavy metal. His long red hair was tied back in a loose braid, something that would eventually become my job to maintain.

I met Roger on the decline. The first few evenings when I came to work, he had me help him into his hot tub, after which I would dress him, then hook up the lift and place him into the waterbed. It was an ordeal, but the process promised to bring him some relief from his muscles, strung tight and prone to spasms. Roger had always been afforded any technology or machinery that could help him function independently, but he had advanced cerebral palsy and his body was nearing its limits.

There were a series of exercises and stretches that he needed me to assist him with. He would lie on his back, and I would put one leg up onto my shoulder and push it toward his upper body. It was part porno, part gymnastics coaching. His already contorted face would twist into agonized knots as he slurred for me to keep pushing. Then I would take turns sitting on his thighs, straightening his stiff, bent legs. Most nights, he would fall asleep with me on his lap, some infomercial droning from the TV next to the bed, the remote out of my reach.

And he coughed through everything. After many bouts of pneumonia, he had a compromised respiratory system and he would hack to the point of vomiting. Nothing seemed to help. It would just eventually stop, and he'd lie there panting from the effort of it all.

At midnight, I could go home. I ached toward those illuminated numbers on his nightstand, littered with cough suppressant, bottles of Gatorade, and empty bottles for him to pee in during the night. My breasts would be rock-hard and full of milk by the end of my shift, and I would selfishly hope for my baby to be awake as I maneuvered through the empty streets toward our tiny apartment. Just to take the pressure away. To soften me enough that I might fall asleep, still hearing, in my sleep, Roger's incessant cough that sounded like dying.

As we worked to get him ready in the mornings, I had to train myself to not ask if he was okay. No matter what coughing, vomiting, muscle spasm that had just occurred, Roger would nod vigorously that he was fine and wanted to move on to our next task, undeterred by physical discomfort that would undo most people. We had more important issues at hand. He relied on me to not only dress him but to make sure he looked good.

"This one?" I would ask, holding up a pressed black button-up shirt.

"Nope. K-k-ke-keep looking," Roger urged me deeper into his walk-in closet, decades of clothing lining each side.

I held up two more, "Either of these?" Vigorous head shaking. No.

"Wh, wh, what, what would your hus-hus-husband wear?"

I thought about Rik and the pile of faded black band t-shirts he pulled from most days, and then the ironed polos on hangers from his short-lived career as car salesman.

"Probably something like this," I assured Roger, holding one up with the tags still on, the fabric heavy and liquid over my hand.

"That's g-g-good then," he relented, as I bent each of his arms and slipped them through the unwilling holes, buttoning the shirt from the second one down, revealing just a hint of fine red chest hair.

Roger was a two hundred pound man, and although it may be unfair to make the comparison, there was something seamless about my days diapering and clothing my infant daughter and my nights spent cleaning up vomit and squeezing his unrelenting legs into sweatpants. Sometimes, I was there until the day's end. Others, just to get him ready for school in the morning. He asked me if I might be able to type his papers if he spoke them to me, and I agreed. I said yes to everything he asked, whether I could or not. I needed to be indispensable to him. Every hour meant another $4.25 on my paycheck.

*　　*　　*

His tract home was near the grocery warehouse. I shopped there after work sometimes when everything but the forklifts had emptied the vast aisles of mealy produce and Spanish generics. At this hour, there was no one around to see me pull out the stack of WIC vouchers I used to pay for our peanut butter, milk, and cheese. Sometimes Roger would give me a twenty to pick up a few things for the next day. Amongst his line of plastic bottled drinks and frozen dinners, I would occasionally throw in a candy bar or Chapstick. I wouldn't tell him and he never noticed.

Was this stealing? By definition, yes. Yet, sitting in the empty parking lot at one in the morning, breaking off pieces of chocolate and letting them melt slowly between my sore-from-grinding teeth, it felt like a reward. A bonus for getting through another day of a life I had never imagined. I told myself, *Roger would give this to me.* He often offered me food or a beer. I never accepted his offers, but I took this as permission.

Sometimes, I stole time. I would add twenty minutes to a shift. Not much, but over the course of weeks, would equal to days. *I've earned this*, was my mantra leaving after midnight, sleeping for a few hours between breast feedings, and then getting back into the car to meander back to that big gleaming house. Tiptoeing in, he would often still be sleeping, and I would fear that he had died. Aspirated in a coughing fit in that stretch of hours that I had gone home. But then he'd shift or fart or just be lying there with the TV on, and I'd wheel the lift to his bed, roll him side to side to place the sling, hook in and begin pumping the handle as if getting water from a well. He would fold into a perfect bundle, rising above the twisted sheets and sloshing bed.

I wasn't the only one who worked for Roger. He had other girls who would do the day or night shift, depending. None of us could work more than twelve hours a week, so I asked for more clients through the agency.

By this time, Rik had been let go from his third dealership and was collecting unemployment. Once a week, he would wake up at five a.m. to inquire about a tree cutting job one town over. Each time they would tell him to come back next week, so he'd drive home and crawl into the California King bed that had been passed down from my grandparents, to my mother, then finally to us. He'd stay there with Sylvia, sleeping, and I would rouse to get to another shift.

Most of the work was bland—helping Joyce, a high-functioning woman with Down Syndrome, to create a budget; making sure Ron got his three-wheeled bicycle to the shop for a new set of tubes; cooking a week's worth of meals for Susan, a fifty-year-old woman blind since birth.

But then there were cases like Martin, who was so large he couldn't wipe his own butt and had stains running down the back of his pants. Porn-addicted and developmentally disabled, he'd sit in his oily tan recliner, a gallon of milk in his grip, asking me again and again if I liked "man and woman love movies." Because the smell was unbearable, the agency arranged for him to take public transport to the grocery store to meet me. I would follow him through the store, listening for his grunts of agreement as I pointed to various foods.

*　*　*

As my clientele was growing, Roger began getting sick more often. He dropped out of school and spent his days at home. I would sometimes stay, off the clock, to watch a movie or listen to some music. It was hard to understand his words, slurred and truncated by gasps and hiccups, but being in each other's company was simple. In this way, I was escaping from home and what waited for me there. There was no middle space any longer, just layers of need and necessity and care, often beyond what I knew to do or to manage. Like Susan's face when I attempted to cook eggplant, soggy with canola oil, bitter and tough. Like the unimaginable softness of her shoulders when she would ask me to rub them for her, little hums of pleasure emitting from her at being touched.

I was running late to Roger's one day, exhausted from being woken in the middle of the night by police. The downstairs neighbors, a reclusive Asian woman and an old man who drove his Cadillac up and down the circular driveway, called the police with a noise disturbance. "There was a report of a baby crying," the officer informed us. We were bleary eyed, holding our rosy cheeked, feverish baby.

"They do that," Rik offered, and they apologized, citing our neighbors as having called frequently on past tenants. I had overslept my usual alarm and I knew that one of the other girls was getting Roger up that day. It would take me a half hour to grab his groceries and head over. I dawdled at the store though, completely unmotivated to face the bottles of cold piss on the nightstand to be emptied, the chunks of dandruff I'd have to comb through to tie his hair into a ponytail, or the crusted toothpaste at the corners of his mouth, waiting to be wiped away.

I was readying my excuse for being late when I clicked the lock and heard shouting. Incoherent and muddled as his speech was, I could clearly distinguish, "Help!"

I ran through the maze of hallways and rooms to find him in the bathroom, crumpled to his knees and hanging by one arm from the metal bar next to the commode. His entire body weight was held by the torsion on his upper bicep and bone, both spare to begin with. I tried at first to work his arm out of the tight space, but I realized quickly that the gravity of his body was too great. I'd have to lift him up and slip his arm out from there.

Not thinking, I held him under his arms and grabbed him in a big bear hug, pushing up with all the strength in my legs. I wasn't strong enough. I could get his upper body lifted incrementally, shifting the point of pressure, but he was dead weight. He said to call 911 and his mother, who lived an hour away. I tried one last time to lift him and felt a terrible wrenching in my back.

The paramedics came and, with the strength of two men, lifted him up and wrested his arm from the bar. I sat on the bed, watching and holding my lower back with two hands, willing myself to stay upright until he was taken away. He was in shock, and from what they guessed, suffering permanent nerve damage. Finally, the house empty, I put the groceries away, left a note for his mother and drove home, wincing with every turn.

Stumbling up the stairs and through the door of my apartment, I made my way to the rocking chair. Rik, surprised to find me home, held a delighted Sylvia out to me. I burst into tears and cried, every sob radiating through my torn lumbar muscles. It was excruciating, but I couldn't stop. Nothing could stop me.

The threshold of my body was one I had not yet met. Trying to make sense of the calculations it took to make a life in close proximity to the needs of others, I had fractured into too many pieces to hold. Rocking myself that evening, ice pack against my back, I wondered how we would keep everything together despite the limits of our two young bodies, no marketable skills, and the mounting responsibilities of an adult life.

My own parents had had me young, not much older than Rik and I were. I remembered falling asleep to the rhythmic tapping of the electric typewriter as my mother wrote her term papers, working her way through college by day and pulling shifts at Montgomery Wards each night. At her graduation, I was as tall as her hip, on which my baby brother was balanced.

I kept working with clients a few hours a week, but I also signed up for classes at the local community college. Sylvia went to the child development center on the days I went to school and when I transferred to the university, she began kindergarten. This is how we built a life, with paystubs and textbooks piled on thrift store tables, each apartment slightly bigger than the last. No high ceilings, but we have a garden grown by Rik's two strong hands and a bed bought solely for us. We worked hard. We were lucky.

Comma Momma

By Kristin Kovacic

1. Use a comma to set off introductory elements.

After over a month away, my college freshman sends me an email containing, in its entirety, her opening paragraph for an essay (probably due in a couple of hours). No need to comment; she wants me to check the commas. It is our only inside joke; she doesn't "get" commas. More precisely, she gets that commas are the *only* necessary punctuation, allowing the harried, headlong writer to separate ideas, go to the bathroom, dramatically pause, enumerate, whatever—commas are like school paste, hastily completing one ring before the next in the brilliant paper chain of her thinking.

She is brilliant, let me not fail to mention, attending a, cough, elite university. She's also sensible and diligent, witty, humane. How terrible is it to have one grammatical fault?

Not very. But I know what you're thinking, you, parent-who-is-not-me. You're thinking she should be correcting her own comma errors. You're thinking, how terrible to have only one funny intimacy between you and your daughter, *one* (count it) joke, after eighteen years of positive, thoughtful, healthy, creative, stable, mindful, whatever, parenting? How lame to get *one* lousy email in a month?

You tell me, chuckling momma. And I know you will, momentarily. I became a mother just in time for the zeitgeist of self-conscious parenting—we stared, compared, wrote books (*guilty!*), blogged, bragged. Currently, we Buzzfeed our anxieties across the wired universe—Are You *Enabling* Your Adult Child? Is 25 the New 18? 10 Signs You're a Helicopter Parent. Or Are You a . . . wait, what's the opposite of a helicopter?

Tricycle? Dirt bike? Wheelchair? Somewhere on the primitive terrestrial level of emotional locomotion is where my daughter and I bust our moves. My cousin and her daughter exchanged 212 texts and seven phone calls in her first *week* at college—in this digital parenting age, there are so many new ways to keep score—but that's not how we roll. We don't talk, much, my daughter and me. We don't text. A grammatical point is the center of our intimate universe. So boo me.

Boo her, too, charging ahead, comma-tose, in her spectacular, mother-free life. I envy her, let me put that out there. I'd like to go back to college, belly-up to the buffet table of knowledge, and feast. I'd like to peek out from behind my shiny hair at the smart and sultry guys peeking back.

But that's a feeling I like to keep separate from missing her. She'd like that, too, and if we had one other joke, she and I, that'd probably be it. *How can I miss you if you won't go away?*

Do I miss her? Yes, no. No, yes.

2. Use a comma to separate the elements in a series (three or more things).

Like you, attached parent, I've spent the better part of two decades observing this beautiful human. I watched while she composed her tiny arguments with me. At two, holding my gaze, she walked *backwards* with the juice she was not allowed to take out of the kitchen, already seeking an escape hatch from the mother ship. First sentences included "You're not the boss of me," and "I want my privacy, please."

She was tough, contained, stubborn, true, quick, observant, thorough—from the very start of life. Unfoolable, she refused all bottles and pacifiers, forcing me to breastfeed until she finally got a cup with her own damned name on it.

From the moment she could write, she liked to bring her universe to order by making lists: Jews We Know; Christians We Know; Ask Mom About. One of her lists, "Rules," composed in crayon during a particularly disastrous play date, virally migrated to copier rooms across America after I taped them to my office door at work:

Rosalie's Rules
1. No telling secrets!!!!!
2. No whining.
3. No phisical contact.
4. No trowing shoes.
5. Listen to grownups.
6. Don't waist electrisedy.
7. Have fun !!!!!!!!!!!!!!!!!!!!!
8. Be nice.
9. Be polite unless your being funny!
10. Always follow theese rules!

My brother-in-law used to begin corporate staff meetings by handing out Rosalie's Rules. In fact, all of us who took this list to work understood that following Rosalie's Top Three Rules—No telling secrets. No whining. No physical contact—would pretty much eliminate conflict. And it was sobering to realize that this insight came from a six-year-old.

My six-year-old. I remember her early bodies. Fine white hair standing straight as wheat on her head. Her fat square foot in my palm. The berry birthmark on the side of her nose, fainter each year. Her delicate frame in a white tee-shirt, pink rosebud on the collar. I was watching, admiring, evaluating—every minute, all the time—like the rest of my friends did with their kids. And for a time, in clear violation of Rule #3, I'd catch her up just to dance with me; she'd kiss me as many times as she could count; I'd knead the warm dough of her after a bath, when we played "Make me a pizza!"

At thirteen, however, she reverted to Rule #3, stopped returning hugs and accepting kisses, pulled up the drawbridge of herself and peered down at me from a high parapet. She was polite (Rule #9), but not funny. I couldn't get a laugh out of her to save my soul (which sorely needed to hear her laugh). It was a long and difficult period, five years of her disciplined, disapproving distance—my girl backing away, still holding my gaze.

In the spirit of Rule #1, I should say that before she was born I feared having a girl, and this is precisely why: this regard. I know, because I was a girl who once regarded her mother from the same high place—with love, but without mercy. I needed my mother in very specific ways (a pumpkin pie, a prom dress, a crisply ironed shirt), but I couldn't, for a long time, talk to her. Like Rosalie, I was never one of those girls *who told their mothers everything.* Yet I couldn't help feeling, over the years of my daughter's childhood, that I should become one of those mothers.

I simply didn't know how. Shamed, I listened hard while other mothers filled me in on juicy news my daughter never reported—classroom antics, crackpot teachers, drama-club drama, teen romances, breakdowns, and bad behavior. I accepted their pity—their daughters dished, while I got my updates from the school website—and internalized their unspoken question: *Doesn't she know her own daughter?*

In the newly empty house, her wee face on a stray refrigerator magnet can slay me.

3. Use a comma + a conjunction to connect two independent clauses.

So I've been getting out more, and today took a walk when no one else thought of it. I had the park to myself, sky quietly blue and the trees starting to riot. A shift in season announced itself in my lungs. As I got into rhythm, I felt my energy rise up to my demand: heart delivering, muscles stretching, bones holding everything aloft. A shift in me, a space in me, opened up. *Here I am*, I thought: moving, alone, separate.

It was a concrete experience, nothing mystical about it. I'll turn fifty in a few days. I've been a woman for thirty-eight years, a wife for twenty-eight, a mother for twenty. My body, me as object in space, has been caressed, ogled, stretched, shoved, squeezed, sized up, sucked, fucked, fondled, leaned on, burdened, stuffed, starved, examined, cut, drained, cleaned, sullied. There have been many hands upon me, hands I love and want to return to. Hands I slapped back (or should have). But this body, and the mind inhabiting it, has been returned to me, whole, completely capable of its animal and spiritual work: propulsion, going on.

And along with the impatient leaves, this other, thrilling idea came down: *No one is watching.* I have my privacy, thank you.

Like most empty nesters and the officially middle-aged, I certainly have regrets. But one of them is wishing for the wrong things. I wished for childhood to be perfect for my kids, not one molecule damaged or opportunity ignored. I wished to be perfect myself—more ambitious, more confident, less judgmental. I wished my daughter and I were closer. But I didn't wish for this—for my sole self returning after a long journey through other lives, other bodies, other selves.

Of course, I wished my kid would get into her dream school, which, in fact, she did. At the freshman convocation, I squinted from the bleachers to pick out the pony tail that belonged to me—my beloved yellow head bobbing in the sea of promise. But the chaplain who delivered the invocation caught me in the act. "These are your children," he said to the flock of proud parents, who, let's be honest, felt we, too, had arrived. "But they don't belong to you. They belong to themselves."

My daughter has been telling me this very thing, in various ways, her entire life. There's a difference between privacy and secrecy, and I suspect that in prior generations everybody knew that, not just six-year-olds. Gathering a new space around her (albeit with a roommate I don't know much about), I think my daughter has been returned to herself, too, untethered, no one looking over her shoulder, however lovingly. That's a heady feeling, I know. In the compound sentence of our lives, we've both arrived at a comma. Something has gone; something is coming, but we're going to stop here a moment and, privately, catch our breath.

Don't judge us, oracles of parenting, friendly rivals I run into at the coffee shop who ask how Rosalie is doing at school. (I don't know; fine, I guess.) We've taken a break from judgment and are composing ourselves for our futures. No secrets. No whining. No throwing shoes.

And in this new, quiet space I hear a faint voice calling from the distance. *I love you, now, will you please, shut up and tell me, where the commas go?*

———

Ashes

By Jon Magidsohn

Late on Boxing Day, well after dark, I scanned the collection
of tools I'd stowed in my backpack to see if I was prepared
for my mission: garden spade, claw hammer, flat-head screwdriver,
keyhole saw, chisel, anything I thought might help whittle away at the
hard soil. If I'd owned an ice pick, I'm sure I would have packed one.
I went upstairs and changed my clothes, convinced my outfit should
be head-to-toe black like in the movies. I couldn't be sure if what I
was about to do was illegal, immoral, or simply frowned upon. Still, I
thought I should try to blend into the shadows, if only for discretion.
I grabbed Sue's canister from the dresser and carried it downstairs. I
put on my black wool coat, threw the backpack full of tools over my
shoulder, and quietly went out the back door. I tossed the backpack
into the front seat of the car and then carefully strapped the canister
into the baby seat in the back. Should I encounter a sudden jolt during
the ride, I didn't want ashes embedded forever in the loosely-woven
Toyota upholstery.

Down at the Toronto Beaches, I parked the car on Lee Avenue half-
way between our old apartment and the new tree, planted two months
before. The tree stood as the closest thing to a gravestone Sue would

ever have. I shut off the engine and sat in the dark stillness of the night. All I could hear were the sleepy Lake Ontario waves treading up to the shore and my breath in the icy December air. I unfastened Sue from the car seat, pulled out my backpack, and closed the car door. I walked with purpose toward the lake, cradling the container in my left arm, until I reached the young sugar maple, proud and lustrous under the nearby streetlamp.

Standing on the boardwalk in front of the tree, I momentarily considered changing my mind. The wall of frozen mist suspended over the shore bore down on me. I looked east into the wind and then west toward the lights of downtown to see if any people were out for a late walk. The coast was clear.

I knelt at the tree, placed the canister on the ground, and removed the small spade from my backpack. One last look around before I plunged the spade into the dirt about eight inches from the tree trunk. The ground was harder than I'd expected; the spade barely made a dent, just a *tink, tink* sound like metal on stone. I reached for the hammer instead and tried loosening the dense earth with the claw end. This proved to be more effective. I scooped out the free soil with my other hand. Clawing and scooping like this for two minutes—I went down maybe four inches—my heart pounded like I was panning for gold. Then I heard voices. I stood up and saw two people and a dog heading my way from the west. I quickly covered the partially dug hole with my backpack and took my cell phone out of my coat pocket. Pacing slowly in front of the tree, I pretended to be just another late-night stroller having a private conversation.

"Yes … Uh-huh … No, no, everything's fine …," I said as the people drew even with me, their dog obediently heeling. "I'll be home soon … I just have one more thing to do."

The interlopers passed by, and I was left to resume my campaign of digging. But I began to doubt my fortitude. The hole in the ground looked like more of a grave than I'd originally considered. Graves are final; irrevocable. Within them, I imagined, people disintegrate. They disappear forever.

I picked up the hammer again and switched to auto-pilot. Claw. Scoop. Claw. Scoop. I worked quickly, nervously. The ground still resisted like frozen rubber, but I persisted. I had nearly reached what I thought was an acceptable depth when I heard the voices of more people coming down the boardwalk. Backpack over the hole, I stood up and resumed my pantomime with the cell phone.

"Hi, it's me," I said. And suddenly Sue was listening on the other end of the phone. "I'm here now, sweetie. I'm at the tree right now ... Can you help me?"

She was sitting comfortably in a quiet, warm, white, dare-I-say "heavenly" place, cordless phone in her hand, listening peacefully to my supplication. She wasn't smiling as I typically pictured her, but rather she had that serious, stern look she'd get when she was fixed on something critical; something she wasn't quite sure how to manage.

"I need you to steady my hands or whatever it is I need steadying." I wasn't sure what I meant by that. I'd never relied on Sue for physical guidance. "We can do this together. Can't we? You and me forever ... And after we do this, I might be able to move forward, little by little." This was more of a question than a prediction. I had no idea how I'd get on from here.

The people passed by, completely ignoring me. I wiped my eyes and looked at the container of ashes sitting at the foot of the tree. Sue told me to keep talking.

"There's so much I want to tell you," I said. "But I'm not sure how. All of my memories are changing color. When you died, so did the future I thought I'd been promised. Without you things are ... blurry."

I looked toward the lake, the frothy white waves fading to distant black. The cold night burrowed into me under my wool coat, but I'd stopped noticing. I thought of the road trip I'd taken with my ten-month-old son the summer before. We'd left Toronto three months after Sue died and crisscrossed North America for six weeks on our adventure of healing, an expedition meant to kick-start my new life as a widower and single father. Being alone with my son and my thoughts brought clarity after the claustrophobic home-grief and it secured a bond between father and son. It also brought to light some alarming revelations that I wished I'd been able to share with Sue. I wondered if I should confess.

"Everything I've discovered since you left is pulling me in a different direction," I said. "I could have spent the rest of my life with you … and that would have been fantastic … but, you know, we might not have made it. We weren't perfect. But I've accepted that … Because that was us."

That was us: imperfectly in love.

"I know you loved me. But … we got it wrong a lot of the time." I swallowed and took a cleansing breath. "If you hadn't died … we may still have ended up apart."

Until then I'd kept my epiphanies to myself, but telling her how I felt was proof that I was moving on; the thick, aching emptiness was starting to lift. If Sue had really been there, she may have protested as she usually did, but I was in control of this one. I looked up the road toward the building we lived in a lifetime ago; before we moved away so Sue could chase down her journalism career, before parenthood, before cancer. Eight months earlier as Sue lay in that hospital bed, I'd said goodbye to her and felt the relief of seeing her out of pain. But now my own pain was lifting without aid, without wondering what she'd think.

"The more I think about it," I said, "the more I believe you would have found some reason to leave me … and I wouldn't have had the strength to fight you."

I still loved her but I hated the memories that had recently become clear. I'd awoken that morning knowing I'd been holding onto the past for fear of the future. And if this telephone conversation was any confirmation, Sue was giving me her consent to let go. But I didn't want to hang up the phone.

"Whatever happens to me from now on, good or bad, it will be because of you. You got me here … and without you, I'll go in some other direction; some other path than the one you and I would have travelled."

Instead of dreading a future without Sue, I realized, I could choose to welcome the opportunities that came my way because of her absence. Some good things could still happen to me. I was thirty-five years old; I still had a lot of life left. Accepting the possibility of a good future wouldn't mean I'd forgotten the life I'd had with Sue. The good wouldn't negate the bad. They would simply be the two sides of one life.

"I have to do this now … It's time."

Maybe this is what Sue meant by life after death. I might have taken her too literally when she spoke of her beliefs. Because I knew she would always live within me. My life evolved with her. Before she came along I was an immature, lazy, idealist looking for a mate. Sue gave me perspective, energy, wisdom and love. She forced me to grow up. She gave me a son. She'd live in him and the person I would become.

I moved over to the hole completely oblivious to whether or not people were walking by. The cold beach had grown peaceful, composed. I could no longer hear the whispering waves.

'This tree will be here forever and so will you.'

I knelt at the hole, the cell phone still at my ear with Sue breathing on the other end. "Okay, I'm going to hang up now … Here I go … "

The calm of night wrapped me in its dark cloak. I looked down at the shadowy hollow I'd mined, pausing in a moment of pseudo-prayer. *I can do this. Everything's going to be all right.*

"I love you … Sweet dreams … Bye."

I put the phone in my coat pocket, removed the lid from the container and lifted out the clear plastic bag holding the ashes. I'd never taken it out before. The volume seemed curiously low and it weighed less than I'd imagined. A bag of sand the same size would have weighed more. I wondered if all of Sue was in there. My cold hands shook as I fumbled with the knot in the plastic bag. For fear of lingering too long, I tore the bag open and tipped it toward the hole in one motion. The little bits of black, grey and white filled it up like water flowing into a bowl. In the heavy, frozen air no residual ash dust came off the empty bag. She was all out. Without pausing, I put the bag into the container that once held Sue and then ladled the cold dirt back over the ashes with my hands. I stood up and packed it down with my feet, firmly enough to level the soil but not so firm as to feel like I was stomping on her. I surveyed the area, making sure it didn't look like someone had just buried his wife in the roots of the tree named after her.

But it wasn't Sue I buried that night. What filled that icy hole was a piece of the past I no longer clung to. Not ignored, just set aside. A past, I'd figured out, that could stay in the past without fear of it extinguishing my future. Eight months of grieving, sadness, hard work, confusion, personal challenges, epiphanies, and loneliness were buried. The tree that sprouted from that struggle stood as a marker in time, resting between what was and what will be.

I packed up my tools and walked back to the car. The icy air filled my lungs and cleared my head. I breathed easier than I had been an hour earlier. Before I stepped onto the sidewalk, I passed a Department of Parks regulation garbage can. The generic canister that Sue had rested in for the past several months had no more symbolic meaning than the lamppost the garbage can was chained to. Sue had always been worth more than what housed her. What had true meaning had been left at the roots of the sugar maple next to the boardwalk. The cheap ceramic container landed at the bottom of the garbage can with a thud.

Picking Up

By Sonya Huber

Stuck in traffic on the Merritt Parkway heading south in Connecticut on a Tuesday morning, I'm staring at the tailgate of a beat-up, black pickup truck in the lane ahead of me. An extension ladder hangs on the struts of a metal support above the truck bed, which is scattered with buckets of tools. The tailgate sports the geometric logo of Narcotics Anonymous and the slogan "Never alone, Never again."

Traffic unclogs, and the green of a New England morning in July blurs past. Even as my car speeds forward, my mind has been hurled backward into to my former life with the sight of that bumper sticker. No—I never met anyone in a parking lot to pay for drugs. I never shook with the physical ache of withdrawal. I just loved an addict. For a long time.

* * *

The addict I loved drove a weathered, blue pickup. When we first locked eyes over coffee, he told me a heartbreaking version of the hard-life stories in own family. I saw a man valiantly struggling to right the legacy of wrongs in the fruits of his family tree. He didn't say, "Hi, would you like to sleep with someone with a substance abuse problem?"

He took me on adventures: fossil picking near a hidden waterfall, a flea market, a drag race. He wrote me notes and left flowers and cooked dinner. As we ate the chicken he'd cooked and ladled from his own crockpot, he told me I had saved him, and I protested. *No, nobody did any saving,* I said. But I enjoyed the stories he told in which I was cast as Wonder Woman. The stories in my own head starred me being good enough, so a cape and invisible car gave me a rush. Plus, he was sexy.

Once, early on, he left me naked on his loft bed for an uncomfortable moment of silence. I heard the tinkering of his drug tools. As the sweat cooled on my body, I knew another love had taken my Wonder Woman status. No—I half-knew she'd been there long before me. No—I had no idea how deep she was into him; she was his origin song, his mother. I pulled on my jeans and ran from his house, and he chased after me. Later, as we walked beneath the oaks that lined my street, he mulled and said, "I should just quit. I've thought about it."

I, for my part, honestly thought quitting was an option, a simple decision.

I weighed and mulled. I sought advice. "He's great on paper," said a sympathetic single friend. The dating pool had slimmed out through marriages, hopelessly twisted personalities, and band guys.

Fast forward years of Googling—is he an addict?—and wondering and diagnoses and indecision about whether to leave.

Because…it was just pot.

So of course I didn't think it was a big deal at all until I got sucked up into a maelstrom and watched as this one life was derailed.

Yes, I have heard about Sanjay Gupta. No, I don't think pot is a problem for most people, but people get addicted to standing in front of a slot machine. This is not even about pot. This is not an attack on your Saturday night or your aunt's legal medical marijuana treatment for cancer. This is about a distant cousin: addiction. If you don't know much about addiction, you are lucky you don't know much about addiction.

I clung to my coffee cup and my to-do list and my furious ability to work, and almost nobody knew. I amped myself up on work and my checkbook balance and the hope of scraping enough together to make Plan B. And we stayed together.

The sordid scenes left me shaking. I could frame the moments with their fractured details, but each postcard of me crying in the night could be turned over to read the secret message: Wish I Wasn't Here With Him. Why AM I Still Here? I was still there—with him. For my own complicated reasons involving hope, my own drug of choice.

*   *   *

Then one day he called me, said, *I can't do this anymore.* The world had crumbled in a friend's back yard, where the summer light made the undersides of the dense trees look like an inverse x-ray, a web of black with light at the edges. A knot had tied in his soul. He touched some electric edge in himself. He told me on the phone that he got too high—even with all his experience, he had crossed into the raw slippery meat of his own brain.

It was a secret day for him, maybe not a day he celebrates now.

I trembled as I waited for him to come home, scared like the waiting before birth or death: he was choosing *us* or maybe *something different that included me.* He saw the outlines of his life as unworkable, which took such guts.

He entered the house with the colors of his face in livid contrast: reds and whites, blacks of the eyes, the mouth. Half of himself had fallen to the inside . He lay on the bed and I was terrified for him. I had longed for this afternoon, had imagined the action in film stills. In the living of it, I was frozen in a strobe light of my uselessness.

More symptoms would come: The creepy crawlies, a splitting headache that triggered his migraines, dizziness and nausea, sweating. Flu-like symptoms and chills. Later, the insomnia and nightmares. Weeks of aggression, blasted thoughts, plunging depression.

We paged through the phone book—tiny letters, thin pages—in a low spot for which there was no 911 to call. This was too common, we learned, and too expensive for 911. I left messages, handed him the phone when I reached the intake nurse. We took turns on hold with cell and home phones, nodding, taking notes, eyeing each other frantically as we heard phrases like "two month waiting list" or "we could call you when we get an opening" or "we don't take insurance." All those private places at the outskirts of the city would be too expensive and too slow. The timing of the crisis and the solution seemed incredibly mismatched. What they didn't say: twenty million people per year in the U.S. needed treatment and could not get it due to cost and lack of beds. We just wanted one.

We found the city option on the cheap: an intake meeting tomorrow and then outpatient meetings during the day and groups at night. He'd stay at home for detox. Work was out of the question. The schedule would keep him contained and safe, with time filled and one place to go. I revered his effort and his guts.

I had hoped for this upheaval, but in practice it a quiet accident, a water leak. No one could know.

One day after he'd gone to group, I sat in the park. I went for a walk where I always walked, but I didn't even make it to the path. I sat down in a kind of squashed kneel in the outfield of a baseball diamond, my calves alongside my thighs, the way kids sit. I closed my eyes and could not even scream. I felt a glowing heat devouring me, not grief but anger in its purest form. The meteor in my stomach weighed me down, too heavy to even carry. Why be angry?

Dumbfounded, dumbstruck: I had not imagined I'd be shattered at being right. I had guessed that this secret might define our lives, but even more secretly I hoped I was wrong. I hoped this phase would pass without a crisis. This was the birth of the next part of our lives, but dirty, like in a gas station bathroom off an anonymous exit.

A friend put me in her car, and we drove past the outskirts of the city, along a highway to a tourist attraction near the town where she grew up. There was an ice cream stand and a goat pen. You could put a quarter into a red metal machine and twist the knob to get kibble to feed the goats with their angular slotted pupils.

I have those flashes frozen like fresh rescue in my head: a goat clambering up a slanted board to reach his neck over the planks of a fence, his lips straining and flapping to reach nuggets of processed food. My hand on his bony back, the bristly fur. Inside the breezy stand with chained-off looping lines like a carnival ride where I stood. I think I bought a shake, and I think it was strawberry. Even as we rode the highway loop, I knew it would end up with me back at home, empty handed, no comfort to offer. In the end, there were times I had to put stuff in the car and flee, just to get out of the way of the unhinging, unspooling.

*　　*　　*

The other addicts mocked him in the meetings, planting the seeds of his relapse as they all ground their teeth and raged with red-rimmed eyes. THC can't make a lab rat's heart explode. God, how those newly clean, irritable, and strained people in chairs railed at each other, raw as pain without skin, competitive about how close they'd come to the lip of hell. Whose hell was better, stronger, faster? The sickest turn on each other, as they will turn on loved ones, rounding on anyone to shred to distract from their own misery.

His counselor met with him privately and sketched out his damage: because he had used regularly before he was fifteen, he was five times as likely to be an addict as your average smoker. Starting early was kind of a cause, but there was always another factor—everything in his young life—that led to smoking up. Call it the genes, the interaction of the drug in the brain, a crushing narcissism, stresses in the home and beyond—new studies even say that the high itself is not what the brain craves, but that the high comes with a dose of doom that only the drug will lift, and the brain yearns only for relief.

We heard figures I had to look up later to understand, the numbers of people unhappily dependent. It wasn't cool to worry about pot, his gateway sweetheart, but we were so uncool now. His drug won first prize, four and a half million no-big-deals seeking treatment per annum.

Rehab and recovery brought us to family meetings where we sat in circles, telling secrets. And I got to see *him*, who he really was behind the chemical screen he'd worn the whole time I'd loved him, and I fell in love twice as hard as the first time. I re-pledged myself to him, then he relapsed. Then again.

* * *

I kept going to group meetings for friends and family members of alcoholics and addicts, and I had to pass the gauntlet of alcoholics and addicts who stood near the church basement's entryway, wreathed in cigarette smoke. They'd nod and say *Hey*, and I'd ignore them. Or worse, I'd give them the look that equaled death. *You demons. You homewreckers, all of you*, I thought.

Not so many years ago, I would see a car on the highway with a recovery message on its bumper, and I'd shudder. I'd send out a prayer to that poor sap's partner, if she hadn't already left him.

We wore our relationship down to nothing and the drugs won, or I lost. Or I won. Or the battle got played out. After I left, I stayed in the groups because they helped me understand the person I had become. I parked in lots next to cars with bumper stickers saying "Never Alone. Never Again." I passed through the smoke-wreathed gauntlet of addicts and alcoholics so often that they began to frighten me less. Then I began to go to some of their meetings to hear them speak. I knew their spouses and kids. I began to see in their eyes a humanity that I had lost the ability to see in my former love.

Now he's still with me in the thousand pop-culture reference to the drug in songs and on t-shirts and in casual conversations. He's with me when I see any of the thousand references to his drug of choice.

Now I accelerate to pass the black pickup truck and turn my head to the right to catch a look at the driver. I am a practiced eye, even racing on a highway in tandem. I see, despite his sunglasses, a posture of calm and a skin color of health gracing the presence of this stranger up as early as I am on this Tuesday morning. I want to roll down my window and cheer him with a hero's greeting, but I settle for flashing him a smile.

———
═══
———

The Pull of the Moon

By Meredith Fein Lichtenberg

I'm watching the water roll in, walking quickly along the shore while there's still land to walk on. I know I could make it around the whole tidal island, back to the wooden stairs set into the rock face, and then up to the summer cottage, before the tide stops me. But I was delayed setting out—by what, I don't remember now: an unexpected load of laundry, a lost Pokémon card, a creeping Daddy Long Legs that spooked my daughter out of her nap.

I walk briskly, but I can't make up the time: I'm three-quarters of the way around, but the beach gets shorter and shorter. Now I'm walking right up next to the rocks. Now I'm tying my sneakers around my neck and water splashes over my feet.

I'm walking faster, grinning as I try to outrun it although I know I can't—it's much more powerful than I am. Now I'm hiking my skirt up to keep it dry, and finally I have to swim. As I ease into the water, I'm laughing that it beat me, and I'm more than a bit exhilarated, hooked. I was ripe for the taking, ready to be swept away by it or by something else.

*　　*　　*

When we first arrived here, we'd driven slowly, the way you do when you don't know the roads yet, where each turn in the road or unusually shaped tree might be the landmark that you'll imprint on your memory. We worried, driving beneath the canopy of old pine and oak trees, that we'd missed a turn—wasn't there supposed to be a bridge?—then the road dropped off abruptly, and a wide salt marsh spread out endlessly left and right: long, waving grass, divided by a gray wooden bridge. Across it, the narrow road climbed steeply into the pine forest, winding across the island to cliffs facing Cape Cod Bay. Only it wasn't an island, just then, because the tide was low.

After we found the cottage, the rest of my family ran to climb down the cliff to the vast, shell-strewn beach, but I stayed to explore the inside. I found that the owners had left us a calendar. It showed the phases of the moon and the height of each day's tides, drawn as parabolic curves along the calendar page. Each day, I saw, as the moon waned to a crescent, the high tide water would surge higher. It would cover the beach to the rocks. It would fill the creek below the bridge we'd crossed. It would overflow whole salt marsh, cover the tall grass, spill onto the pavement, make the road impassable, at first for minutes, but then longer and longer each day. By the new moon—they called it the "astronomical high tide"—the road would flood for hours, cutting us off from the bridge, the rest of the Cape, and the world.

*   *   *

Vacation is always lulling and maybe a beach vacation even more so, but this cut-off place that's drowned twice daily makes me feel almost drunk. Since the road floods at inconvenient times, and I'm not a planner, we rarely get off the island. I never get away from it long enough to come down, so I keep feeling all I want is more. It is enjoyable in a way that feels a little naughty, like a cocktail hour that goes on for weeks.

In the hall, there's an aerial photo of the island. I can make out the pitched roof of our cottage, a speck of reddish shingle visible through the knot of pine branches and scrub oak. The Bay water swirls around like a Van Gogh, but the colors are blurred, so you can't tell whether you're looking at water or sand or marsh. I pore over the photo, and the tide calendar, and my maps, obsessively. I don't want to think about anything else.

I take down the photo, and soon I'm carrying it with me from room to room. Each time I look at it, hungrily, it's like I'm taking another hit. This was how I was when my kids were infants: they cried, or even just peeped, and I became dopey with the strength of the call, impelled to respond to it. I was obsessed with their rhythms, disinclined to get far enough away from them to sober up and see it more clearly. This didn't happen the instant they were born, of course; at first there was the shock at what I'd lost.

But when that subsided, it was obvious: my babies' needs were clear, irrefutable. When they needed, simply, my breast, all I had to be was the breast they needed. It made me docile. Every time I looked at them, I was drunk with it again. It wasn't just that I was broken, or that my instincts rose up and I saw I was perfect for the role just by being a mammal. It wasn't even that, as the weeks passed, I did it for the sake of the love growing between us. Yes, it was those things, but more than that, living so completely constrained by them, living utterly in their minutes, there was so much about me that I did not have to decide. It was heady. For a while, I could be simply a mother with her young, fecund, legitimate, uncomplicated.

* * *

When the tide comes in, we walk down to the bridge and see teenagers who gather there to jump into the cold Bay water. A handful of skinny boys with farmer tans goggle at the curves that half a dozen sunburned girls are trying to camouflage under shorts; their play-acted confidence is punctuated by giggling. When the intensity peaks, they all jump off the bridge to cool off. Wading in the marsh, collecting green crabs with my kids, I'm aware that I have all the freedom the teenagers imagine they want, and even access to adventures they haven't dreamt of yet.

And, yet, I am spending my vacation at the one shelly beach near the cottage, snacking on stale bunny-shaped cheese crackers because we're out of peaches and the tide too high right now for me to cross the bridge and drive off-island to the farm stand. I'm not restless. If I stay here, in sync with spring tide and neap tide, it will shape the day for me. And that feels, at the moment, perfect. People talk about freedom like it's only a good thing, an ideal, the ideal, but it's also so damn demanding. This feeling of containment—we can't leave because the tide's in—takes the pain of decisions away; it's easy to surrender to it.

Surrender is so unlike regular life. It's not *maybe we should stop using plastic wrap is it worthwhile to buy Ad Words for my website do you think we should talk to your parents about getting long-term-care insurance I wonder if that conference is a good networking opportunity or a waste of time, and by the way who might I be in this life I'm making?* Only, simply, *yes, now, for you.* Regular life has freedom. But there's a different liberation in being defined, for a while, by something bigger than you—the ocean, the infant's hungry mouth. It made me happy for a long time.

This summer, for the first time since I last looked, Henry and Jane are not babies. Being fundamental to their hourly survival has, I realize, long since given way to lovable, fungible parenting. There is time now to attend to questions of plastic wrap, Ad Words, long-term care insurance, networking, other things. But I'm soft and used to surrender. There's a vacuum where babies' rhythms once defined me. In the vacuum, I reach for something else to contain me, to numb me, to let it stay simple a little longer, and in flows the tide, also gigantic, demanding, beautiful, and simple. It carries me along, willingly.

I walk around thinking "water." Water. Water and water and water and water and water and what more would I want and I'll be the island and let it suffuse me, shape me, create me. I feel I am helpless for it, that sparkling feeling that takes over, makes me feel something-like-happy, and a little dumb. I just want to think about it again and again, to be near it and let it command me and keep out all the other big stuff. I feel I am in love with the rhythm of the tide. And is that so weird, really? I was also, twice, in love with babies who were, then, little more than mouths, lungs, and assholes. They were my flood and ebb, and I loved them, and I love this.

*   *   *

Somehow, though, one day, we venture out to see friends. We return home late in the evening, sleepy, and as the car comes over the hill, I literally gasp to see the marsh, spread-eagled, careless, before us, and island rising up beyond it, awaiting inundation. The bridge is dimly lit by a handful of stars to the east and the last bit of sunset to the west. Water is everywhere, and I'm so instantly pulled back into its magic that it takes me a minute to realize that we misjudged the timing. It's half an hour before high tide, but already the pavement is wet. A man with binoculars tells us we can't cross safely till the tide turns and water ebbs away. His shoulders are low and his feet are in waders. He speaks in a slow, authoritative cadence. "The road dips down on the far side of the bridge. Even if it's still passable here, it's too dangerous on the island side."

I blink dumbly, repeatedly. "We have to wait?" I ask.

Greg quietly suggests we leave the car and hike home in the dark, and some tiny fraction of me briefly imagines us wading across and climbing through woods lit only by a merest sliver of moon. It's what we'd have done before the kids. But Henry worriedly asks what we'll do, and Jane observes that it's very dark. I am as slow as a cow, disoriented, but I can see that she would need to be carried and he would complain all the way back. My habit of surrendering doesn't lend itself to adventuresome thinking.

So we wait. A long, cranky hour passes in the car. I open the windows and look out at the stars and the marsh. Even in darkness, I can see the water moving in; I can hear it, moving towards me, relentless.

The kids respond to long periods of confinement with a kind of hideous duet—each takes solo verses to opine about the injustice of having had to share the one good fishing net all day, or our present lack of snacks and entertainment. Then they come together for a complain-y, bickering chorus that would sober anyone up, their voices joined in harmonious resentment. It is my least favorite sound track.

I think of whole days trapped with them—hundreds of them— with a toddler insatiable for endless rounds of *The Erie Canal* or a preschooler smelling every dog-piss-fertilized flower on the way to the store. How lovely it had been, at first, to surrender to them each time, to find their helplessness or curiosity thrilling, their appetite for repetition fascinating, clues to the people they'd grow to be. And yet sometimes I spent—I spend—a whole morning waiting for naptime, searching among my feelings for the peaceful surrender that came so naturally at first. Sometimes I find it again. Other times I feel, *I want my fucking freedom.* But motherhood deadens your impulses. You don't leave a little one behind. You don't even fantasize about it. You look at her and she pulls you back in and the restive feelings are all against your will.

The high tide finally rolls in and then begins to recede dreadfully slow. I am itching to get moving but I'm so tired. The sea's undertow pulls some kind of crazy love out of me, undeniably; I don't wish it away. It is irrational, the way it's irrational to love being your babies' bitch. But right now, strung out on the tide we're tied to, I want to go home.

*   *   *

On the day of the new moon, we finally join friends off-island, at the ocean. My toes sink in to the loose, white sand dunes there. Compared with the packed, moist Bay beach near our cottage, it's hard to walk. The sun blazes, reflecting diamonds all around me, so bright that I'm confused; between the glare and the deafening surf, it seems our island is a cave we have hibernated in, and now, away from it, I'm jolted awake by hunger, amazed to reencounter the world—it's huge and beautiful, and I've been asleep for years.

All at once, it's evening. The idea of folding ourselves into the car, back to the cramped domesticity of the cottage is unbearable. I am suddenly ravenous. I want French fries and onion rings and fried oysters and stuffed quahogs, a baked potato with a little plastic container of sour cream and beer on tap and soft-serve ice cream. I want everything you can't get at home.

We end up at a local place with a hundred other vacationers in skin tones ranging from sunburnt to roasted. We share a long picnic table with someone else's bickering family. The kids, restless and whining, draw on paper placemats with broken crayons, and solve the word-find with the improbably misspelled "seafod." The adults are clutching plastic lobsters that will light up and vibrate, eventually, to let us know our order is up. It's too bright, too loud, hard to wait. Everyone is cranky, and I don't feel like trying to make it better. I think, longingly, for a moment, of our tidal island, dark, limited, yes, but also a buffer against these harsh wilds of Tourist Restaurant Hell. It is a nest whose beauty makes me so dopey I call the drudgery of cooking and cleaning and caring for my little ones a "vacation."

My life is that nest. I designed it to fit my peculiarities, to comfort me so I could brood and nurture my young and learn to be their mother. I placed each leaf and feather and twig painstakingly, then filled it with people I love. It limited my world, so I could focus on theirs. I made it so beautiful that living in it seemed like a terrific deal in exchange for my time, my body, my freedom. It was, once.

In the loud restaurant, now, everything seems distorted, pointed the wrong way, poking me; I have no room. This life I've so carefully built, loved ferociously, found so much more than satisfying, this nest, which suited us so well, it's not just a nest, anymore. It's a cage. And its bars, woven all around me, are the twigs and scraps I chose myself, placed with my own hands and heart, according to my own design, to contain me. The kids are hatched now; it's only me still hoping to be comforted by containment—grasping at anything else that reminds me that for a brief time there was a role that suited me so perfectly I was willing to enslave myself.

My cheeks are hot with shame. Even birds, with their almond-sized brains, know that after the little ones hatch and fledge, it's time for the mother to fly, again, too, to go anywhere, alight unsentimentally for sleep on any old twig. Even the most lovingly built and well-used nests are just for a sojourn. Only human mothers try to remain there so long that they go crazy. Only human mothers could try to stay in a cautious, protective role that fits less and less, a little longer, a little longer, to avoid seeing the loss, the heartbreak of being outgrown, the terror at what we might become next.

A while after the plastic lobsters vibrate, I want to get going. The high tide isn't until late. "But it's the new moon," I say, over and over, more to myself than to anyone. But Henry and Jane dawdle with French fries, and on the way to the parking lot there's *No we can't do mini-golf tonight* and *Fingers do not belong in your brother's ear* and *Let it go, she said she was sorry*. I gun the engine restlessly while everyone straps in.

Off the highway, I fly up the road with the pine canopy. I take the hill so fast that my stomach springs up to my throat and down to my groin. As we crest the top, I see alongside the marsh, several cars parked and slow-moving folks wading down to the bridge or standing, hands-on-hips, gazing into darkness. They're here to see the astronomical high tide.

The water is already creeping up the road, farther than we've seen it before. In a wordless, agonized split-second calculation, Greg and I meet eyes and realize we'll be trapped here till midnight.

I open the car door to see water already inches up the tire. It is closing in. It's not *containing* me, *holding* me, *providing me the structure I need*. Not anymore.

Our eyes meet again for a moment as I make the decision. Then I drive forward, not testing, tentative, but lurching, foot to the floor. The water is deeper than I had guessed, the steering wheel not so responsive. But my foot is an anvil. The world dwindles to nothing except for my certainty that I must get across immediately. The car is listing to the left as we descend, deeper, towards the bridge, and it occurs to me that I could miss the bridge entirely and go straight into the creek. I think: *I must get through this motherfucker!* And then: *This mother really may be fucked.*

I'm loony, I think. But it's moonless tonight, and I'm the opposite of loony: I'm emerging from a years-long dopey haze, and now getting out of it, I'm newly reusing a muscle I can only barely control. My pacing is wild. All I can think is that I must drive forward.

My aim is decent, and we're up on the bridge, momentarily on dry ground, and I'm elated. We're halfway there. We thunder across only to descend with a belly-flop splash to the further side. The causeway here is deeper, and for a moment, I can't quite feel the pavement; are we floating?

My head is roaring, a chorus telling me to GO! GO! GO! Water is splashing over the hood of the car (GO!! KEEP GOING!). I need to turn on the wipers (GO!). It's so dark that I can't see where the road ends and the marsh begins. Are we veering left? If the tires go into the marsh, we are sunk (FASTER!). I can't see the road at all (DON'T STOP! KEEP GOING!). There is no road (GO! GO GO GO!).

I hear Greg's voice, as through a tunnel—is he telling me to slow down? I am afraid to listen, afraid that whatever he says will be like the newborn's cry, like the rising tide, a Siren's wail, tempting me back to the habit of following, surrendering, but I am in the driver's seat now. We all need me to jam the pedal down and go forward, with no compass and no way to steer, navigating only by the imagined road ahead.

Then I'm on dry land, heading up the hill onto the island, speeding, now that I'm not dragged down by feet of water. We whip along the sand road, through the trees, the last mile through the steep forest.

Shaking and triumphant, I'll be sore tomorrow, but for now, I'm laughing uncontrollably, giddy. I feel soaked with tears and sweat; adrenaline races through my arteries. Soon all four of us are whooping and giggling. At home, we put the kids in bed unceremoniously, still covered in beach and dinner, and Greg and I walk back down to the causeway without a flashlight. The pines above look like pulled cotton balls against the black sky, and the moonless night is so dark we navigate purely by memories of where the road curved or bent or rutted. We walk without speaking, dumbfounded, holding hands, and arrive exactly as the tide is high. The marsh is so full it looks like a lake, covering even the tallest grass, deep enough to reflect us, and the trees from the island and even the stars above. The sky and the water go on and on, even farther than I can dream of.

———————

Getting Ginger

By Michele Coppola

My ex-husband died and left me his dog. It wasn't an official bequest, but since all of his friends claimed to love her to death, really, but just couldn't take her in, I drove five hours south to pick up the rickety Staffordshire terrier named Ginger who we had rescued together ten years prior.

"It's wonderful what you're doing," said my ex-sister-in-law when she called me. "I'm sure Marty is smiling down on you."

Not likely. The first time he'd gone to the hospital in liver failure, I'd texted him and asked if he wanted me to come down and get Ginger— but the only response I got was second hand from a mutual friend. He said that even though Marty knew he wasn't able to care for the dog properly, he'd be damned if he was going to let me take her away.

"Alcohol is what's taking his dog away," I'd said angrily. "The same thing that's taken everything away."

* * *

Ginger had been our first foster dog when I brought her home from the shelter a decade ago, her hopeful eyes looking up from a skinny, dun-colored body dangling with exhausted nipples. Confiscated from a home where she'd already been bred twice, the last go-round resulted in nine puppies that had drained her completely . It hadn't been hard to do since she'd barely been fed and had nothing to drink save a puddle of muddy Oregon rainwater. Marty and I were in love then—with each other, and with the idea of turning our three-acres-and-a-trailer into an unofficial dog rescue.

After several weeks of fattening her up and teaching her a few commands, we re-homed Ginger with an affable long-haul driver, who took her on cross-country adventures and fed her truck-stop meatloaf. It was a fine life for a sweet dog. But a year later, a bad accident on the interstate took the trucker off the road for good and brought Ginger back to us, also for good. Once she was again curled up on our couch, Marty and I found we couldn't part with her.

"Animals were also close to McGuire's heart," read the article about my ex-husband's death. At one time he'd been a popular DJ in the small town where he'd lived most of his life, and his passing made the front page. He was indeed an animal lover, poetic and soulful, with a malleable heart that never seemed to recover from the blows and dings that come with daily life. We were immeasurably compatible, and when we moved in together, we didn't spend the weekend unpacking; instead, we used our rent money to take a road trip through Northern California, pulling off at scenic overlooks to make out and licking fast-food barbeque sauce off each other's fingers. Tunes from an old Allman Brothers' CD completed the new love movie montage.

Eight years later, he refused to look at me as we sat in our second marriage counselor's dim office. "I'm not giving up alcohol for her," he said. I felt my face flush red—not with anger, but with embarrassment. How lousy a spouse was I that my husband wouldn't even consider sacrificing a half rack of Milwaukee's Best to keep me? I remember wanting to protest that I'd cooked all of his favorite meals whenever I had the time and that when my face wasn't mottled and puffy with crying, I wasn't half-bad looking. But I didn't. Instead, I moved into the other bedroom and told him I wanted a divorce.

*   *   *

That memory still cuts me as I reach over to the passenger seat in my car, where Ginger is now coiled into a petrified ball. My hands smell like french fries and old socks after I pet her—just like the house where Marty had been living. It's been seven years since I tearfully agreed to take our three other dogs to Portland with me and let my ex have the member of our canine family most likely to never leave his side. Ginger is fourteen now. When I tried to put the leash on her back at Marty's house a couple of hours before, she hid behind his roommate. Finally I got her to come to me and I stroked her ears, something I remember she always liked. Still, her expressive brow was wrinkled with worry.

I'm a little worried myself. My current husband Bryon isn't happy about having a third dog, but I have promised him that I will find Ginger another home quickly, something I already know will be nearly impossible. He and I squabble frequently; you can smell the dependability and routine on him like a nose-burning aftershave, and sometimes his rigidity is beyond exasperating. While he likes animals, he certainly didn't want a house full of them. But he did want me, and I come with canines that bark when a squirrel sneezes and a cat that sleeps on his head. He never swats her down in frustration, though. He gently lifts her from his face and places her, carefully curled in the same position, at the foot of the bed.

We argued about Ginger the night before I went to get her. "I don't mind you going to get the dog. I understand that," he said. "What I don't like is all the baggage that comes with her."

"What baggage?" I asked, wiping away yet another large, infuriating tear from my clammy cheek.

"Yeah, what baggage," he said, turning back to his laptop. "Go. Do whatever you need to do."

I hate like hell that nearly every emotion I have comes out in tears. I don't miss my ex-husband; during our marriage I slowly realized that this was how it would end for him and it's why I left. And yet … there is something so profoundly sad about the way Marty slowly deteriorated in the last few years, like watching a fragile sandcastle that took a whole afternoon to build get washed away in the tide. But I still wasn't prepared for his death when it happened, and now Bryon looks at my downcast eyes and thinks I'm hiding remnants of an old love. What I'm actually trying to conceal is the fact that I am beyond angry that after all of this time my husband thinks I could still be carrying a torch for my ex, and also furious that Marty was in such deliberate denial about his condition he wouldn't make arrangements for Ginger, the companion he swore he loved more than anything in the world.

Back on the road, I stop for a sandwich at a drive-thru outside of Roseburg. I tear off a meaty corner and offer it to Ginger, who sniffs it warily, then buries her nose back in the dirty crocheted blanket that had been on Marty's bed back at his house. I took it so that the old girl would have a familiar smell to comfort her, and also because I recognized it as one I had made for my ex many Christmases ago. Just one more thing from the past I'm dragging into the present that my husband and I will absorb because it's what we do. We are boring and stable and responsible.

And yet, I am immensely appreciative of the fact that I have a working vehicle and the gas money to come rescue Ginger and a comfortable home where, until I find her a permanent situation, she can spend her days snoring contentedly on the couch. These resources are at my disposal in no small part because of Bryon, the man who has already called me twice to make sure I'm doing okay on the slick mountain passes. I feel reasonably sure that if the situation had been reversed—that I died and Marty were called on to come get a dog we'd owned together—he would have been both unable and unwilling to help. Not that he wouldn't have regretted his impotency; in fact, my guess is it would have taken at least an entire bottle of booze before he didn't feel bad about it anymore.

The sky is a watery blue-gray when I pull into the driveway of my house, the sun resigned to another day behind clouds. Ginger sits up in the passenger seat and shivers. I can barely breathe when I think about having to convince some reluctant person to take her in and then leaving her there to curl up in the dark corner of a strange-smelling place, leaving her to wonder why the man she loved so much didn't want her anymore.

*　*　*

"So we have a third dog now, right?" says Bryon, who is sitting on the bed smirking and rubbing Ginger's belly. It's been two weeks since I brought her home, and in that time we've discovered that in addition to being somewhat deaf, my ex's dog is a bit incontinent, requiring potty breaks every two hours. Unfortunately, she is also petrified of the doggy flap, so we must get up and let her out several times a night. My husband doesn't complain about it; he just rolls out of bed and stumbles to the back door with a sigh. I'd be happy to do potty duty, but Ginger wakes him up when she's got to go; she sleeps on the floor by his side of the bed and follows him to the kitchen, where he feeds her bits of the flatulence-inducing cheese that she loves.

"Well, no, I'm still working on it. I posted her picture on Petfinder," I say halfheartedly.

"Oh come on. Who's gonna want her? She's old, deaf, has to pee all the time. But she's such a good *guuuurl*," he purrs into her floppy ear. Ginger rolls over on to her back and snuggles her grey muzzle into his lap. She attached herself to him immediately when I brought her home, and if I'm being honest, I felt a twinge of resentment. Dogs live in the moment, so it's entirely possible she didn't remember me at all—but apparently she knew instinctively that Bryon, with his understanding eyes and strong, warm hands, was someone to be trusted.

I get up and wrap my arms around him. "Thank you," I whisper. I love him so much for this, for the absolute conviction that society will start to unravel if he doesn't step up, for believing that dismissing this dog to become someone else's problem is just wrong. That is what Bryon does—even when it's exhausting, even when I tease him unmercifully about his Eagle-scout code of honor and wish he could just relax, already. What I didn't realize is that it's hard to lighten up when you're made of such sturdy stuff.

Perhaps Ginger knows what I am just learning: that in the end, love is really about showing up, again and again and again. I was there for her. Bryon is there for me. No matter where I step in this marriage, even out to the edges of his tolerance and my good sense, the floor is sound; there are no soft spots, no decay. It will hold me up, even with the added weight of my ex-husband's elderly, incontinent dog.

Fear and Rafting on the Rio Grande

By Zahie El Kouri

We have paddled beyond the point of return.

I am in the left front corner of a rubber raft. The guide has told me that if I jam my leg into the groove between the outside air chamber and the one that makes the floor, I'm less likely to fall out of the raft, so I jam my leg so hard that my left butt cheek aches.

The guide, who is almost certainly stoned, decides to do a safety check. "Everyone raise your oar like this."

He holds his paddle up vertically, with the wide side toward the water. He does it with a sort of swagger, like this job makes him much cooler than scared city girls like me. I mimic his action precisely, clutching my oar in fear. My husband and his sister do the same, with confidence. My sister-in-law's partner Dawn holds her paddle up, too, but she holds it horizontally, so the wide side is facing the center of the boat.

"I said *this way*," the guide repeats. "You need to look at me." The guide is sun-leathered and rangy, his hair bleachy-blond.

"I can't look at you," my sister-in-law says. "I'm blind."

This statement comes as no surprise to me, and it shouldn't come as a surprise to the guide either, as we'd discussed Dawn's blindness with him when we arrived.

We're on the Rio Grande, the five of us: my husband John, outdoorsy and fearless; his sister Liz, a four-foot-ten Krav Maga instructor; her partner, Dawn, an executive with a Manhattan non-profit; and me.

I am full of fear: I am afraid of heights; I am afraid of riding a bike in traffic; I am afraid of getting a concussion while skiing like I did when I was eleven. I generally don't talk about my fears like a Woody Allen protagonist, but I try to avoid situations where I put myself in what I perceive to be danger. The more rational part of my brain tells me that lots of people go rafting without injury and that I have reached an age where I am willing to give this kind of risk another try. Nonetheless, I am happy for my helmet and my life jacket, and even though I have lost all feeling in my left leg, I jam it further into the raft.

Since neither Dawn nor I had ever been rafting, we signed up for the beginning level trip, a leisurely float down the calm part of the river. When we arrived, though, Liz and Dawn snuck away to change our trip to the intermediate one, which included something called "class three rapids." I am terrified, but I don't want to ruin everyone's fun. Dawn, on the other hand, is smiling, her legs casually resting on the floor of the raft.

The guide says, "Well, just pay attention." When we approach the first set of rapids, I paddle as hard as I can, against every instinct I have to curl into the fetal position. When we're clear of the rapids, I see that everyone else in the boat is smiling, while I'm just happy to be in one piece. The next few rapids are the same—fear for me, smiles for everyone else. After the fourth set of rapids, we float along the river for long enough that I am able to take in the greens and browns of the riverbank.

That's when I notice the large boulder in the center of our path. It is taking up most of the river, but it looks like there's just enough room on either side for us to get by. Water splashes up the rock and churns around it in a great white frenzy.

"That's a big rock," I say to my husband.

"Yeah. Which way should we go?" he asks the guide.

"Oh, we're just going to bounce off that thing," the guide says.

"Bounce?" I squeak.

"Just paddle as hard as you can right up onto that rock, and then we'll bounce off to the right."

This does not sound like a good idea to me, but I am a lowly city girl who can't feel her left leg. The rock looms ever closer, and I paddle as hard as I can straight on top of it. My corner of the raft hits the boulder. We bounce once off the rock and land sideways, the right edge of the boat hitting the water.

I am still in the boat! Hooray!

I look to my right. The seat next to mine is empty. John and Dawn and the guide are all in the water. Liz is leaning over the side of the boat, holding Dawn by her collar. John erupts from the water and climbs back in, his leg bloody.

"Dawn's in the water," I shout. The water swirls innocently around the raft. John jumps back in the water, helping Dawn clamber back in to the center of the boat, soaked and grimacing.

The guide lifts himself into the raft.

"Y'all took a swim?" the guide asks. "Get a little wet?"

Dawn grumbles.

"Dude," the guide says, as about to share the wisdom of the ages. "It's all about facing your fears."

Dawn whips her head around to face the direction of the guide's voice. "I do enough of that taking the subway in Manhattan every day while *being blind*."

The guide says nothing. John and Liz turn away from him, back in their places.

Dawn stays in the center of the boat, shaking. "Is she going to stay there?" the guide asks.

"Yes," says Liz. "She's had enough."

The guide looks at John, alone on the right side of the boat.

"*Dude*," he says, "you'll have to paddle harder."

He says it to John, but I take the message. We launch again, and I paddle with a new determination. Dawn has navigated New York City blind for thirty years; now she is thrown from a raft in the middle of the Rio Grande and climbs back in. Who am I to be afraid?

———
———

Into the Woods

By Rebecca Stetson Werner

Dear Lucy,

I wrote this story for you, but when I began it I had not real-ized that girls grow quicker than books. As a result you are already too old for fairy tales, and by the time it is printed and bound you will be older still. But some day you will be old enough to start reading fairy tales again. You can then take it down from some upper shelf, dust it, and tell me what you think of it. I shall probably be too deaf to hear, and too old to understand a word you say, but I shall still be

your affectionate Godfather, C. S. Lewis.
Introduction: *The Lion, the Witch and the Wardrobe*

I am packing for several days away from my family, away from my husband, Jonathan, and our three children. I am going to spend much of that time in a hospital, I know. I am preparing for this by carefully considering what I will need and what I need to leave behind. I stand before my closet, my Wardrobe, and consider my options. I pull out two skirts. They strike me as nicer than my typical jeans and perhaps they will somehow help me feel more comfortable, more grownup, more respectable in the hospital world I am about to enter. Maybe

I'm reaching for a fur coat as I pass through the Wardrobe and into Narnia.

I move from the closet to my nightstand and gather my laptop and cell phone and coil up their power cords. I take several folders and books of work I am in the midst of. And then I grab a book of fiction, thinking I might have a lot of time on my hands, and I toss it into my shoulder bag. The one I grab is from the pile of middle-grade-reader books I have recently collected from the library for Julia, our daughter. Books that expose young readers to the world outside their family, with themes of the difficult but doable, dark but with a promise of a happy ending.

Julia and I are working our way through this stack, both of us happily devouring the stories. So perfect for her because she is nine. So perfect for me because apparently this is what I need right now. As I enter this new stage of my adult life and grow up a bit, and I reach for the fairy tales of my childhood to help me walk through this new terrain and find a path through the dark forest. Just as C.S. Lewis promised. They are my sustenance right now, and, like a gingerbread house, they have me enchanted and captivated.

So. Two skirts, a cell phone, and a child's book to keep me company during a very adult journey. I register the irony, and also how it seems just right.

Somewhere within me, down deep, I know. I know it is very important what you select for a journey. In your bag will be the only things you will have when you face problems, uncertainties, riddles, witches, and wolves. What seems random, what seems thrown in for another purpose, or by chance? Could be what you trade for your very life.

At least that's how it works in fairy tales.

*   *   *

As with all great art, the fairy tale's deepest meaning will be different for each person, and different for the same person at various moments in his life. The child will extract different meaning from the same fairy tale, depending on his interests and needs of the moment. When given the chance, he will return to the same tale when he is ready to enlarge on old meanings or replace them with new ones.

Bruno Bettelheim, *The Uses of Enchantment*

My father has been gone from the hospital's surgical waiting room for quite a while. Really, for a long while. Though I am not sure this is actually true. It feels as though I have been here alone—alone but surrounded by strangers who are separated from me by their own internal struggles and worries about their own loved ones—for hours.

My mother is in surgery, a minor surgery, a surgery resulting from her age, a "tune up" as we explained it to our three children when I told them that I was going to be away for two nights in order to be with Grammie in the hospital. I am here just in case. Here to keep my father company. Here to try to make sure my mother moves more easily through the complicated sequences of hospital care. Here to get her home as quickly as possible.

I have come to that place in my life: I am caring for my own children, big enough to not need me at all moments of the day, but often needing me more, needing me to be figuring, wondering, considering with them in more complicated ways. This time of tending my children blurs and overlaps with the beginnings of tending my parents. Helping them out here and there.

And then, my father returns to the waiting room from a trip to the bathroom and from a walk out to the car to find something to pass the time. He gives me a small smile and walks over to our chairs with his lopsided gait, never quite having regained his surefootedness after his knee surgery a few years ago. He eases into the chair beside me and says, "I should have left a trail of breadcrumbs. I got a bit lost."

I look at him, assessing his seriousness.

He does not seem upset. If he was lost, he seems to have handled it. And then, I look down at my hands in which I'm holding the fiction I grabbed as I packed at home. It had remained tucked away in my bag until, alone in this room, I had dug it out in order to help me ignore the pain and sadness of the people around me, to drown out the daytime talk shows blaring on the TV in the corner of the room. To hold my gaze so I could give myself and those around me a sense of false privacy.

Its title? *Breadcrumbs*, by Anne Ursu.

In this moment, I realize that this book is my Floo powder, my portal between two worlds. My magic beans, my potion in a vial, my key tied around my neck opening the last door I need to pass through. From the moment I started to prepare for this journey, and really for every moment, every major event of my life, there is a steady undercurrent of story. Moving like a river that guides and explains, flowing under the surface of real life. These fairy tales and children's stories—with their themes and roles and relationships, their adventure and struggle with maturation and separation and needs and desires. They are told to us when we are young and are here with us in every conscious moment. We retreat to them, draw upon them, quote them, and use them between us as a shared experience and vernacular to guide us.

Fairy tales, given their oral storytelling origins, hold common truths. In fact, they must. For in order for one narrator to decide to pass them along to another, tales had to have been deemed *good stories*. Had to hold themes and roles and problems and resolutions that resonated with their audiences. They were told again and again until eventually they were written down. And then read again and again, until they became a part of our cultural history, and of our personal narrative and compass for our own lives, internal and external.

I look over at my father, my former woodsman, to see if somehow he knows, if he is referencing my book's title. But he is not and does not know that I am reading this modern fractured fairy tale. He is instead listening to his own internal map, relying on the network of story that is within him as well, trying to make meaning, trying to understand these unfamiliar woods by following the rules of those storied woods he does know and has visited before. Hoping that perhaps he will know what to do now.

He and I have been adjusting ourselves to each other in these past hours, figuring out who sits and who stands near my mother during admission. Who gets the first kiss goodbye as my mother is wheeled off to surgery. Who answers the phone when my mother's name is called in the waiting room. Who pays for snacks from the cafeteria. Who is in the lead and who is following behind on this path. It used to be him leading, always. But today, as uncomfortable with and as ill-suited to the task as I may feel, I think it may be me. If my father is not the woodsman, then I may not be the little girl anymore. Even if these woods are dark, and the nurses and wolves are scaring me a bit.

My father, as many do who reference this story, seems to have forgotten that the trail of breadcrumbs was faulty. On their first trip to the woods, Hansel cleverly drops white pebbles to lead them home. It is on their second trip that he uses breadcrumbs, his only available material, and these impermanent, edible, and disappearing trail markers are what ultimately cause Hansel and Gretel to get lost in the woods, unable to return home. Only then, faced with this problem, does Gretel rise to the occasion and lead the way on her own self-determined path to their happy ending. Somehow it is troubling to me that my father has forgotten that we don't want to leave breadcrumbs, that what he needs is something more permanent. And inedible.

So far? *My* role is to hold things. I have placed my mother's car keys in my shoulder bag next to my cell phone and have tucked her wedding ring, the one they snipped off her finger in case there were *complications*, into my change purse. Before I did so, I checked the engraving. The nurse had not cut through the inscription, my parents' initials, followed by the date of their wedding. Somehow I am relieved. And like any fairy tale, each item I collect has some kind of meaning, some kind of purpose, each statement a window into underlying wishes and needs.

*   *   *

This is what happens on journeys—the things you find are not necessarily the things you have gone looking for.

Anne Ursu, *Breadcrumbs*

My phone vibrates, a text from my brother. He is at work, a doctor, several states away. He hasn't heard from me. My father and I have been waiting here for six hours for what we were told would be a three-hour procedure. I have not texted my brother for a while with an update. Because I am trying to sit still, trying not to move. Movement might be interpreted as panic by the imaginary wolves of possibility in the room with me. I am waiting for some information. I have been hoping not to have to send a message admitting that I have no idea what is taking so long. I know right now where my father is, but I have lost my mother for a bit.

Despite the states separating us, my brother and I are here together in this new place. Trying to figure out how to make this shifting role with our parents work. And how it will work between us. Because we are still the same people, the same children. We are still on the same path, walking together, he the older brother, me the younger sister. Our roles, our history, the story of our childhood together cannot be ignored as we take these next steps.

My trickster brother, my fellow backseat rider, has grown into a brilliant and successful adult. He actually saves lives on a daily basis. In his role as Hansel, his focus is on the world in front of him, and he moves through it with strength, skill, and confidence. He expects, as darkness falls, for the white stones he wisely laid earlier to begin to glow, to keep us safe, and he expects to know the right thing to do.

I'm not sure he would ever leave a faulty trail of breadcrumbs. That's my role. I am much more likely to leave behind a trail of the accidentally vanishing variety, birds eating the crumbs and making our way home impossible. And this mistake would not shock anyone who knows me. I have been given the role of observer, wanderer, emoter, but rarely leader. My ear is more likely pressed to the forest floor, listening to the rumblings and undercurrents and meanings that are held beneath the surface of the action above. When I try to walk the path that Hansel would blaze, I trip and stumble and get lost, because this is not my role and not the path I would choose for myself. But with my lifetime of poorly chosen materials, I am afforded the ability to laugh at myself and not be very surprised to find myself lost in the woods because I was listening to the rhythms below, with no plan for getting home. I look about the room. It is relatively empty. There is no one to ask for directions.

Some time later a nurse and then a doctor come to tell us everything has gone well. My mother is doing just fine and is in recovery. I am relieved. And a bit angry at the doctor for the frozen fitful slumber my father and I have been plunged into for the past three *extra* hours. I ask a few questions. My father is quiet but asks for reassurances that she is okay. My mother's doctor looks tired. I try to forgive her. I tell her I hope she can go rest for a bit. She looks taken aback. I realize that this was not the thing to say here. She is the one doing the caring.

We are told we have another hour before she will be ready to be transferred to her room. I tell my father I will be right back, and I go to the bathroom. I text my brother and Jonathan from the stall. I need a few moments of aloneness with my relief.

I emerge and go to wash my hands. I look at myself in the mirror. I reach up to my hairline and pluck a grey hair from where it has been sticking straight up toward the florescent lights. I stare at my reflection for a few moments before another person enters the room.

Mirror, Mirror.

*　　*　　*

She had done her best to be prepared, but had not anticipated crazy people.

Anne Ursu, *Breadcrumbs*

Despite all my preparation, packing, and collecting along the way, I had not expected to get into an elevator with my mother, pale and scared looking, still under the influence of anesthesia. Nor had I anticipated where this elevator would take us.

"Did you and Dad get some breakfast?" she asks when she sees me walking toward her. Despite the drugs, she knows her role, her lifetime as the Baker. I feel comforted that she seems lucid. This is a very typical question from her. I answer that yes, we have. And glance at my father. *Should we tell her we've had lunch, too?* I wonder through my eyes at him. He does not answer. Unlike in fairy tales, we cannot apparently speak with our minds.

I squeeze in beside her and hold her hand, lifting my large shoulder bag above the railing of her bed. I turn to her. She is focusing on me. Staring at me. The attention is unsettling. I crack a few jokes and then swallow more, realizing that the recovery room nurses in this incredibly small space with us might see my retreat to being silly as inappropriate. Or more likely, as the rantings of a heartless mad woman. My father is silent, making himself as skinny as possible, standing behind my mother's head. I am not sure she knows he is there.

"I think I might be talking funny," my mother says thickly, as though her face is numb and her tongue non-responsive. And then, "Did you and Dad get some breakfast?" Her eyes grow wide, and even more scared as I answer that we have. And lunch, too. "Did something go wrong? Am I okay?" She's garbling the words.

Her vulnerability is dawning on me. I respond by being overly cheery. I explain to her what the doctor told us, that it just took longer than they had anticipated, but that there had been no complications. I start trying to be funny again. My father can't hear me. My mother is loopy and confused. The recovery room nurses just look at me. I am babbling.

"Did you and Dad get some breakfast?" she asks for the third time. I turn to my father, who either has not heard her or is really good at hiding his reaction. Are we trapped in some small circle of time together, sleeping in this moment for eternity while the rest of the world moves on without us? Or maybe I am just being childish and this is just something that happens when Moms come out of anesthesia?

This hospital. I was born here. And as if to make this all come full circle, I follow my mother's wheeled bed out of the bank of elevators and onto the maternity ward. "Ah," I say, "this is where we met." I say it mostly to myself. But my groggy mother and her recovery room nurses look at me with equal amounts of confusion and concern.

"Critics who treat 'adult' as a term of approval, instead of as a merely descriptive term, cannot be adult themselves. To be concerned about being grown up, to admire the grown up because it is grown up, to blush at the suspicion of being childish; these things are the marks of childhood and adolescence. And in childhood and adolescence they are, in moderation, healthy symptoms. Young things ought to want to grow. But to carry on into middle life or even into early manhood this concern about being adult is a mark of really arrested development. When I was ten, I read fairy tales in secret and would have been ashamed if I had been found doing so. Now that I am fifty I read them openly. When I became a man I put away childish things, including the fear of childishness and the desire to be very grown up."

C.S. Lewis

Once we are settled into her room, we focus our efforts on the same things that I imagine my mother and father focused upon when we were last here all together forty years ago: eating, sleeping, and pooping. I notice families outside her door taking their first walks in the halls together, babies pushed before them in wheeled bassinets. I see lactation consultants come and go. I watch some newborns being cared for in the nursery. I run into tired fathers in the kitchenette downing coffee. I think of my children, and of my now-woodsman, Jonathan, to the north of here. And turn back to my parents.

I order my mother meals on the phone and I take my father for a third meal in the cafeteria. On my mother's ward, *the* mothers' ward, we pass by the newborn nursery at its center. I see myself there as a baby and see my own children being given their first baths in nurseries very similar to this one. I quietly register that I am now like my mother in another way: there will be no more newborns for me.

My mother is struggling with her lack of control, of being the one who now needs tending, and her mood is rolling in unexpected waves. As she wakes from her long slumber, we are cast as children, then as evil step-parents, pulled in and then pushed away. Her eyeglasses now returned to her, she holds them up, looks at me through them and then not through them. With glasses. Then without. Over and over. She sees me blurred followed by invisible, and I am not seen well in either case.

I step out and go for doughnuts. I nibble from the gingerbread house for a bit and bring back treats to my parents. Upon my return, I once again enter this shifting, muddy, dim terrain populated by the where and who and when we are, and by what we packed and who all of us have been up to this moment. We crash and bump and collide into all of these selves in the room together. The Woodsman and Gretel, the Snow Queen and the Gingerbread House Woman, the wolves and the birds. Hansel is on the phone, asking me about medications for which I do not know the names. I try to make light, but know that I should have asked about this already. I would like to talk to him about how full and noisy and messy it is here in the room with all of our past and present selves dancing about like wood nymphs. But I don't. I just go find a nurse to answer his questions.

The chaos in that room. The spilling and boiling emotions. The things that have been felt and seen and said. My instinct is to talk, to process them, as I have awkwardly attempted to do throughout the day. But I choose to hold them instead. And not just hold them, but bottle them, thrust in a cork, and pop them into my bag. That is something I can offer all of us. For now, I will keep my awareness to myself so we can all continue moving forward together. I can wait to press my ear to the ground. I can choose to just keep walking.

*　*　*

Now, the world is more than it seems to be. You know this, of course, because you read stories. You understand that there is the surface and then there are all the things that glimmer and shift underneath it. And you know that not everyone believes in those things, that there are people—a great many people—who believe the world cannot be any more than what they can see with their eyes. But we know better.

Anne Ursu, Breadcrumbs

Finally, I am heading home. My mother is doing well. My father is at the helm. My brother will be here later in the day. We have our happy ending. Yet I know I have now entered unfamiliar woods. And that I am going to have to walk around in them for some time now. And contend with the rustling noises.

When I get to my car, I notice that I have a message. From my father, to whom I have just said goodbye a few minutes before. I dial voicemail and set my phone on speaker. I begin my long drive back to my children, hoping to meet them outside their school, to hear about their days.

I just got outside and noticed there is a steady sleet coming out of the sky. The temperature is hovering at freezing. But as you drive north, it may be slippery. I don't think it is going to accumulate, but I wanted to let you know. Please drive carefully.

The Woodsman has returned. So I grab a bite of Turkish delight. Feel the fur coats brush against my face as I pass back through the Wardrobe. Flick the reins of my Subaru. And head north, toward home.

Lucky Girl

By Jessica Handler

I was in my late twenties, on a road trip with friends, when I flopped into a chair at a music club in New Orleans and had a look around. We were lucky; the club was rocking, and we were already in a highly pleased state from visiting the drive-through daiquiri place. When I caught sight of a trampled baggie trapped under a table leg, I leaned down to examine it, making as if to tie my shoe. The bag had either been hidden for safekeeping or fallen from a stoner's pocket. If it held a few loose joints, I'd take it. If it were pills, I would take them only if I could identify them. This bag held neither. The bag held a jackpot: leathery, grayish chunks of psilocybin mushrooms. Lucky me. Free drugs. The baggie was in my pocket in a flash. Later that night, the mushrooms met orange juice and a blender, and then my body.

This moment in drug history is more than twenty years old, but it's one in a sequence that composes a kind of mental flip book for me. There are the "first acid trip" pages, which end with a teenaged me supine beneath the comic book spinner rack at my neighborhood pharmacy, whirling the cosmos of *Archie* and *Weird Adventure* above my head while belting out a then-current Three Dog Night hit. I like that sequence; it's funny and poignant, the stuff of memoir. I'm also fond, in a rueful way, of my memory of origami-style birds fashioned from the cut-off corners of magazine pages. The glossy paper made neat packets to hold just enough cocaine for a few pre-party lines. I'm less affectionate toward the next pages in my flipbook: me licking the empty, unfolded paper triangles, searching the creases for remnants of the numbing thrill.

"We'd have a hard time getting you addicted to anything," my physician mused during a recent checkup. She'd prescribed a short course of something innocuous, and I'd balked. "I'd rather not," I'd told her. I wasn't afraid I'd become dependent: I'd already done my obsessive turns with better drugs, and years had passed since I'd licked, swallowed, or pocketed anything that rated as a Class IV narcotic. I was tired of drugs, prescription or otherwise.

"You're lucky," she said.

I grew up sneaking peeks at the *Physician's Desk Reference* the way other kids steal a look at the *Playboy* magazines their fathers believe are safely hidden behind the laundry hamper. The PDR's color pictures of pills were my idea of erotica: pale pinks, blues, and greens, sweetly side by side or blatantly aggressive in grainy blow-ups. Most of the book's scientific language escaped me, but I welcomed its atmosphere of danger tinged with hope. My father got a new *PDR* every year, hardbound and heavier than any of the Martindale-Hubbell law books in his office, and nearly as thick as the dictionary in our den.

He believed he needed them. My two younger sisters were terminally ill with separate diseases; their illnesses were moving targets, and every drug might be a door to redemption. On Sunday afternoons, I went with him to the pharmacy (later the location of that first acid trip) to fill sheaves of prescriptions and buy a carton of his unfiltered cigarettes. Sometime between his first and last trip to the drugstore, my father developed an addiction to amphetamines. Eventually, my mother was knocking on the pharmacy's glass door before business hours, meeting my sisters' needs for real medication and filling my father's illegal scrips. She didn't know then that he'd had them faked, only that she wanted his rages stilled so that she could mother her daughters in moments of peace.

My friend Suzanne theorizes that people our age don't do recreational drugs because we no longer have the leisure time to recover like we used to. That Captain-Crunch eating, pajama-wearing indolence of the next day—and even the day after—lives in a spot on our personal timelines when no one needed looking after (those mirrors laid across table tops weren't tools for self-reflection), and grocery-buying and bill-paying were afterthoughts at best. "We're afraid we'll run out of luck," I agreed. "We're old enough to know we could die."

Even when I was young, I knew that luck stuck to people in different ways. Even though my father was an addict (who didn't buy his drugs on the street, and was therefore, a different, better class of user) he was also, for a while, the executive in charge of an alternative sentencing drug treatment center. The basic algorithm at the center: go to state-sponsored hippie rehab, or go to jail. Junkie teenage run-aways only a few years older than I was slept in the center's bunk beds, washed the spaghetti-crusted dinner dishes, and were encouraged to chime in during "rap sessions" led by social workers. On the few occasions I accompanied my father when he dropped by work on a weekend, I made a beeline to a reasonably clean beanbag chair beside a dirty window. The air smelled like musty old house, incense, and dirty socks. I'd bury my face in a book and try not to breathe.

My father excelled at the complicated handshakes the inmates—earnestly called "family"—bestowed upon him. Some of the older boys in the "family" looked dangerously romantic to me, aloof, and thin as pin-joints. I imagined hanging out with them, impressing them with how much I knew about their twin passions, drugs and rock music. I was eleven. I had no idea what we'd actually do or what their lives were like. Hiding behind my paperback copy of *The Exorcist*, I stole periodic glances at the wall clock, counting the minutes that became hours until my father and I could go home for dinner.

At home, drugs hummed in my sister Sarah's nebulizer. The motor made our kitchen smell vaguely of plastic while she coughed through the vapor. Drugs had swollen my sister Susie until her face resembled a wheel of white cheese. Drugs were all around me, close as family, distant as adulthood. Two more *PDR*s came and went before I gathered pills and pot from my father's bedroom bureau and made friends in high school: gentler, less-broken versions of the unapproachable treatment-center boys.

*   *   *

My flip book didn't end in New Orleans. Not too terribly long ago, my husband and I stood in the doorway of a coffee bar in Amsterdam, reading the chalkboard menu. We felt awkward; buying pot in the open in order to smoke it in the open seemed utterly wrong. The prices were suspiciously cheap. Turned out they make it up with the lighters. Inquiring *puis-je utiliser votre Zippo?* of a French twenty-something at the next table got us smoking. My husband, a soft-spoken, deep thinking man, had told me a raft of funny college anecdotes about pot turning him into a deathly silent, withdrawn shell. "I get really quiet," Mickey said, drawing out the "really." I'd stopped smoking pot years before we met, and the harder stuff was long gone from my life. My husband and I had never smoked together.

In the coffee bar, I smoked one joint, delighted that they roll them for you. They box them, too, like my Camel cigarettes of yore. I smoked and talked. I got garrulous. I sang along with the stoner video for "Little Green Bag" playing in a loop on the television in the corner. I lit another. I chatted with the folks at the next table. And Mickey grew quiet. Really quiet.

"Honey, are you okay?" I asked, pretty sure that he wasn't.
Silence.

"Honey, do we need to leave?" I had three entire joints left, neatly rolled, in a cute box. The coffee bar was plastered with signs warning me not to leave the premises with marijuana. Our hotel was plastered with reverse messages: bring any marijuana in, and face imprisonment.

My sweet husband moved his head. Not a nod, but a barely perceptible vertical bob.

"Can you stand up?" I asked. Please be able to stand up, I thought, eyeing the vertiginous spiral staircase to street level. Mickey made that same head-gesture and, as if he were emerging from a puddle of glue, rose to his feet.

Un cadeau, I said to the French kid with the Zippo, pointing to the box with my last three joints. Lucky him.

Step by slow step, my husband and I climbed the metal stairs to street level and walked carefully to our hotel, each snow-dusted cobblestone and trolley track a massive obstacle.

When I told Suzanne that we're old enough to know we might die, I was thinking back to Amsterdam and my history of fearsome chances: a beloved husband rendered mute in a basement coffee shop four thousand miles from home, a reckless young woman churning dubious flora into a blender, a desperate mother negotiating a momentary balance. And what I see now in that mental flipbook are brushes with danger, and a few very lucky people dancing on the edges of something close to hope.

———
———

A Gift for My Mother

By Amber Stevens

My mother called today to tell me her dog died. She spoke in halting, measured tones; she expected me to be devastated. I should have been. After all, I had loved that dog and had chosen her myself from a motley litter of neglected pups shivering in a hole in some asshole's backyard, a piece of plywood thrown over the top for shelter.

"Twenty bucks for her," he'd said, then spit a stream of tobacco by my shoe. "Hell, take two. Ain't got room for 'em pups. Second goddamn litter this year."

I glared at him. I was fifteen, fearless. These puppies were no more than four weeks old; I could see that. The one I chose would probably be the only survivor. I scooped her out, a trembling golden pup with liquid brown eyes, a gift for my mother, although I was really the one who wanted a dog. Her belly, pink and soft, thrummed against my palm; she mewed like a kitten. I shoved money at the man, muttered thanks, and walked home with that tiny, trembling body tucked in my coat. I loved her already, of course. Her uncomplicated love would fill a void for both my mother and me: for me, she would provide affection and acceptance, and for my mother, she would be the perfectly yielding and submissive creature she'd longed to raise.

When I left home nine years ago, fleeing cool mountain air for desert sky, my only regret was seeing that cocked head poised at the front bay window, watching me drive away. I couldn't explain to her that I wouldn't be back that night, or the next, or maybe ever. She had slept piled on my feet for four years, but she was technically my mother's dog. I'd driven away and left her there and, after a few days, stopped imagining her sitting at the window waiting for my return. It's a talent I have. Out of sight, out of mind. But I did know this, from conversations I had with my mother over the phone, when conversation with her was still possible: the puppy I'd once rescued from a hole in the ground had grown old, couldn't run anymore, couldn't climb stairs, had gone blind in one eye, and suffered from bad hips. So maybe that's why I didn't cry. I knew it was just her time to go.

With my mother, it wasn't so easy. I pictured her on the other end of the line, frowning, broken heart warring with bruised ego, waiting for me to offer her some form of compassion, or break down in tears, or anything to flood the dam between us. I could hear her questions in the silence. *What happened? What did I do?* I was grateful for her pride, which I knew would protect us both from the answers. She would never ask out loud.

*   *   *

"Molly died," I told my husband after dinner. Greg was at the kitchen sink, scraping leftover mashed potatoes and corn into a large coffee can. We'd recently begun composting, determined to transform our nutrient-depleted soil into something that could nurture a garden. That had been my idea. I had visions of sprawling zucchini, tomato plants with plump red fruit, flowering broccoli and crisp lettuce, thriving under the fierce desert sun. A garden against all odds. I soaked the hard ground and split it open, battling dry, unyielding earth with shovel, sweat, and stubborn will. I spread bags of musky fertilizer, breaking soft clumps against my gloves and sifting them through my fingers. I picked out stray bits of gravel and turned the soil until it was like silk, shaping perfect, even rows for sowing seeds.

The whole family planted together. My seven-year-old daughter methodically placed each seed according to the measurements on the packages, gently pressing a fresh layer of dirt on top. My son, who was two, dumped his seeds in a pile and brushed them roughly across his row, brow furrowed in concentration. Greg sprayed a fine mist of water across the plot, and we smiled at each other, hopeful. We watched the water sink in the ground, watched the ground deepen into rich, fertile black. The wet earth released pungent waves on the evening breeze, and the kids groaned, giggled, and pinched their noses.

Greg peered over the stove. "Who died?"

"Molly. My mother's dog."

"Awww. That's too bad."

He came back into the dining room, where I sat shoving food around my plate. The kids had already bolted to the backyard, Anne scattering bubbles across the lawn for the benefit of her little brother, who chased them maniacally, collapsing in laughter as they popped in his chubby hands. Greg leaned against the patio door and watched, grinning. "Look at those two. A ninety-nine cent bottle of detergent and they're happy as clams. We could have wrapped some bottles for Christmas and saved a few hundred bucks."

"Mmmm."

He turned to me. "What's wrong?"

"I told you. Molly died."

"She was pretty sick, wasn't she?"

"Sure. But still." I pushed my plate away. "She was kind of my dog, you know, before I left home." It was an accusation.

"You never told me that. I'm sorry, hon." Greg tipped his head and smiled gently. "I'm sure it was for the best."

I looked away from his sympathy, hating it. It felt better to chastise him instead of myself, for feeling nothing. I was a wonderful person. I stared past him, at our children playing. Anne stood like a gazelle, her legs long and graceful. When she had slid into the world, slick and purple and showered in blood, my heart had swallowed her whole. How exquisite, the relief that swept through me as I clutched her tiny body to mine, gasping at the final expulsion of my pregnancy and all its secret fears. *You can love a daughter*, I'd thought. *You can be a good mother. There is nothing wrong with your heart.*

*   *   *

After Anne was born, we flew north to the little town nestled in the mountains where I'd grown up. Anne was my mother's first grandchild; I wanted to give her every chance to form the bond with her granddaughter that had somehow eluded her with me. *Perhaps the baby will even bring us closer*, I thought on the plane. I imagined the hard lines of my mother softening as she watched me stroke my daughter's smooth round cheek, sponge her tiny body clean, and swaddle her in soft towels; I imagined my mother gracefully relinquishing control and accepting her role as a grandmother.

The visit had been hell. She swooped in like a bat, folding Anne into her black embrace that was always more possession than affection. She pinned the baby against her shoulder while she stormed through the house collecting laundry; she clucked disapprovingly at Anne's outfits, bundling her in blankets and whispering loudly to her husband, Tom, "The poor thing must be freezing!"

Tom would wink at me and shrug his shoulders. My anger at her dissolved into pity, for him. How could he stand it? But of course, he loved her. They had met and married shortly after I'd left home, eloping in Vegas in a move that shocked everyone. This woman who had never tolerated anyone. Tom was a good provider and she was able to quit working as a housekeeper; she took a part time job at a bookstore, spending her days quilting and working on her home. I was grateful that she had found someone she could live with; it relieved my burden of imagining how I would ever care for her later. It's difficult to say who would be more miserable.

One morning on my way to the coffee pot, I glanced out the window and saw my mother feeding Anne a bottle of breast milk. She had spread a blanket on the grass and sat with the baby cradled in her arms, pressed against her bare chest where her button-down shirt fell open. Skin to skin contact. So Anne would know her smell. My stomach turned and bile burned my throat. *You had your chance*, I thought. I wanted to run out there, snatch my daughter away, and never return. Instead, I went back to bed, flinging myself down on the mattress she'd fitted with sheets from my childhood. I should never have come back here, I thought, and I began to cry, feeling all the ground I'd gained since leaving home shift underneath me, knocking me down.

*   *   *

She'd come to visit us several times since then, alone; Tom hated to travel. The pattern was always the same. We began cautiously hopeful, skirting the landmines of each other's egos. She lavished praise on my housekeeping, my children, my career. I stayed up longer than I wanted to, listening to her plans for the garage shelves, the arguments with her neighbors, the peace she finds in her rose garden. How badly I wanted to love her. In those first days, we even shared secrets. She once confided her recent lab results, and how she woke the next day facing her own mortality. I once admitted to feeling like an inadequate wife, never completely at ease with an ironing board or a skillet. We smiled at each other, tentative.

By the third day, our smiles had worn thin, and all efforts to reach each other receded in mutual irritation. Her compliments would grow louder, thinning and tapering into sharp points that punctured the air, her sincerity popping like a balloon.

"It's so smart that you let Matthew eat whatever he wants! They're only little once, so what if they're chubby? It's so cute at that age!"

"Anne certainly has her own mind, doesn't she? My goodness, what a feisty thing! I guess the less you discipline your children, the better off they are, right? So they're strong, independent. Yes, things are different now, and I'm sure it's for the best."

Only I understood her. My husband was oblivious, and my children didn't recognize sarcasm. I remembered the secrets I'd shared with her, and I felt embarrassed and angry for giving her more ammunition. Soon I was slamming cupboards and taking long walks at night, carrying on imaginary conversations where I politely told her to go to hell. I didn't have to say anything; she knew. When it was finally time for her to go, she would ask Greg to take her to the airport, and we'd stiffly nod our goodbyes on the porch.

The guilt set in instantly, a churning in my belly, a fist around my heart. I pictured her at the terminal, sitting stoic, jaw set, wiping away angry tears. I cursed my weaknesses. What would it cost to indulge her? Why couldn't I take the higher road? In another six months, I promised myself, I'll try again. I'll invite her down, and we'll watch *Anne of Green Gables* and *The Sound of Music* and go out for huge, dripping hot fudge sundaes and swap our best salsa recipes.

And so I would invite her, and she would accept, and the goddamned trip would be just the same. Until the last time when everything changed.

When my mother called to tell me about her dog, I hadn't seen her in two years. My husband had stopped asking, but of course, Anne persisted, fueled by the lovely, blind innocence of children. "Why doesn't Grandma come anymore? When can we see Grandma?" I kept telling her, "soon," hoping the knowledge would one day sink in and leave me blameless, like the truth about Santa Claus.

* * *

I stood to clear the table, glancing one more time at my son, chasing rainbows spun in soap bubbles that burst on the grass. I saw the breeze shift, saw the bubbles suddenly change course and drift toward the garden.

"No!"

The dishes clattered back to the table; I threw the patio door open just in time to watch Matthew crash through the freshly cultivated plot, crushing onion stalks beneath his knees as he tripped. His arms flung out, his fingers driving through the dirt and ripping out several newly-sprouted carrots. He stared at their exposed, spidery roots, then looked up at us, uncertain.

"Bubba," he explained.

"Oh, honey." I stepped gingerly between the rows, scooped him out, and brushed the dirt from his clothes.

"It's not his fault," I said to no one in particular. "I meant to get a little fence up." Matthew twisted away and raced back to the yard. I knelt at the edge of the garden to survey the damage, careful to avoid my husband's gaze. Warm tears were slipping down my cheeks and I dabbed at them with my sleeve, feeling ridiculous. Here were my baby carrot plants, torn from their cool, dark shelter, where their roots had already begun to spread hungrily. I picked one up and gently placed it back in the ground, securing it with a fresh mound of earth, hoping it might survive. Greg knelt beside me and began to do the same.

We worked quietly together as the sun began its slow descent and cast honey-colored shafts of light across the patio. I felt his gaze pass over me like a shadow. He had learned not to ask. After several years together, I still didn't know what you could and couldn't share with a husband. No one can hear the whole truth of a person, and not walk away.

Later we made love in the dark, and after, the tears came again. I sat up and pulled my knees to my chest, wrapped my body in the blanket. I told myself it was time. In the dark, I wouldn't have to see his face.

I told him about the last time she came, right after Matthew was born, when Tom came with her. I told him how one day, when I turned the water off in the shower, I heard Matthew screaming from the bed. I told him how I rushed into the room, laid next to my baby and nursed him, dripping water on his cheek. How I jerked the sheet over my naked body when someone knocked on the bedroom door, and then entered. How Tom paused at the bathroom door, then turned back and asked if he could watch. "I've never seen a woman nurse a baby before," he'd said, and I thought it was all right, he'll just look for a minute, and I was covered up, the baby latched on.

I told my husband how I wasn't prepared when Tom sat on the bed and found the baby's leg under the sheet, how I was too shocked to protest when he began stroking Matthew's leg, rubbing my thigh in the process. I told him how my throat locked, and it seemed like it went on forever but it was probably only a minute and then the baby let go and my breast was exposed, wet with milk, and Tom gasped and then he stood and walked stiffly to the bathroom without saying a word.

Greg was silent. And then he said, "But are you sure he—"

"Don't," I hissed. "Don't you *dare* question me. That's why women don't tell. But I'm telling you. A woman *knows*."

Later, Greg held me under the bright lights of our kitchen. He stroked my hair. He asked me what I wanted him to do.

And I told him. Nothing. Because she needs him more than she needs me. Because their marriage is worth more than our fractured relationship. Because it's too late for her to start over. Because I think the best gift I can give her is to let her go.

———

Fertilizer

By Susan Rebecca White

Back when I was still shell-shocked from having separated from my husband of nearly seven years, when we still had a massive amount of financial untangling to do before we could truly own our own lives, when I was still kept awake at night by waves of panic about not having enough money to support myself, a friend told me, rather matter-of-factly, that I had a pile of shit in front of me that I had to eat. Not only that, but all I could use to do so was a tiny spoon. The good news, she said, was that one day I would reach the end of the pile, and then much lovelier things would be placed before me.

Her prediction turned out to be correct. I met Sam just as my divorce finalized. I like to say that he was my prize at the end of all of that shit, like the toy buried at the bottom of a box of Cracker Jacks— except of course, that's not fair to the Cracker Jacks or to Sam.

When Sam and I first started dating, I was subletting a small carriage house in my native Atlanta. The carriage house was built in the 1920s, had hardwood floors and French doors, and the walls were painted a cheerful yellow. Sam lived about a mile away, and since we both worked from home, sometimes I would fix pimento cheese sandwiches and invite him over for lunch. He would bring sweet tea.

After we ate, we would take a walk around the neighborhood before we both returned to the more practical details of our day. One sunny spring afternoon, after our walk, Sam and I tumbled into bed—work be damned.

We were thirty-six and forty-one years old, and we were in bed together on a Wednesday afternoon, sunlight streaming through the blinds and making stripes on the quilt. It was hard not to feel as if we were getting away with something. This was not what most of my friends—in the middle of marriages, careers, and parenthood—were doing. Yet Sam and I were not cheating on anyone, were not making up excuses to our bosses, were not neglecting our children. Both divorced without kids—his divorce more graceful than mine—we had each eaten our fair share of shit to get to where we were, in the giddy stages of early love. It was heaven.

After dating for nearly a year, Sam and I took a trip to Panama, snorkeled over undulating jellyfish, kayaked in the middle of the blue, blue ocean, gripped each other's hand as our cab driver weaved recklessly in and out of Panama City traffic. Back in Atlanta we celebrated our one-year anniversary by having spaetzle at the same Alsatian restaurant where we had our first date, and it was there that Sam proposed.

By the time we married in a tiny ceremony in our home with a homemade cake and a bouquet picked from my friend's garden, I was thirty-seven, Sam forty-two, and we wanted to have a child. Given our ages and our level of commitment to each other, it was tempting to start trying on our honeymoon, but I had a novel coming out the next month, and a tour to go on, and I didn't want to be distracted by the "am I/ am I not" game one inevitably plays while trying to conceive. And so Sam and I waited until my book tour was over in July. At the end of that same month, seven days before my period was due, I took a pregnancy test and was rewarded with a faint blue plus sign.

I felt incredulous that this—pregnancy—was happening to me. I had always felt on the outside of things, a consummate observer. For a long time, this was my preferred mode of being—it gave me an illusion of control that I desperately needed. Agonizing over choices was infinitely preferable to actually making them. Which is why I spent much of my first marriage trying to figure out whether or not to have a child. It was far easier to wrestle with that question than to face the truth of my situation: that I was in a marriage that no amount of therapy would fix, and that I had willingly put myself into this untenable position in order to avoid fully committing to life, with all of its vulnerabilities and uncertainties.

I am now nearly nine months pregnant, my belly big and tight, my energy low, my body taking on a life of its own, and subsequently doing all sorts of embarrassing things. When I sneeze, I pee! When I walk ten feet, I get winded! If I don't eat a bowl of prunes every morning, I'm constipated! Despite the all too earthy side effects, I love being pregnant, love that I get to experience the bizarre and amazing process of reproduction. I love feeling our son roll and kick inside me. The sheer physicality of the late stages of pregnancy makes what began as something abstract (revealed only by mild nausea and a plus sign on a pee stick) into something much more real. And the realness of the pregnancy has brought me closer to the astounding prospect that we will soon have an infant to care for. That once I deliver the baby he will be in our charge, and I will somehow learn to breastfeed, and get by on little sleep, and grow more patient as small tasks become mighty endeavors. Soon there will be a human manifestation of our love—living, crying, and pooping among us—and we will love him in a way we have never loved before and will consequently be more vulnerable than ever.

Still, I am not yet a mother. I am intellectually aware that a mighty and miraculous wrecking ball is about to smash up the life we know, but I do not understand this on an emotional level. How could I before our son arrives? And so I find myself suspended between the life I knew and the life I am entering, much as I was when I boarded the airplane that took me away from my first husband and our home together and into a future yet known.

This means I am acutely aware of what I am losing: right now Sam and I are still a two-person unit with a host of inside jokes and allusions. We are newlyweds and we are playful. Hopefully we will remain playful as parents, but there is a weight that will come with our new responsibility that we cannot ignore. Post-baby, we probably won't spend many Sunday afternoons playing Ping-Pong at the local sandwich place. Most likely I won't cook as elaborately as I do now. Cheese soufflé will no longer be on the rotating menu, nor will I make homemade soda syrups and granola bars. We will have to watch ourselves and not act horribly toward one another when sleep-deprived and overwhelmed with the stresses of new parenthood. Chances are, we will not always succeed at doing so, and our own warts and shortcomings will be more fully revealed.

We are trading one reality for a more intense, harder one—one that for us will be richer, and deeper as well—and we are both ready and excited for the change. And yet the other day, I found myself weeping over what we are losing, our sweet courtship of pimento cheese sandwiches and afternoons in bed. I found this unsettling: it felt like my old, non-committal self coming back into play, the woman terrified of getting herself into something she couldn't get out of. My tears also felt disloyal toward my unborn son, whom I already love with a startling ferocity. But then I tried to be gentle with myself, the way a mother might be, to allow myself to be sad about the ending of this time when we know each other only as a couple, this time of burgeoning love among people who are not new to life, who weathered some hard things before meeting (and who will surely continue to weather hard things as life goes on). I imagine that twenty years from now, I will think of our early, heady days as a couple with sweet nostalgia. And probably also with a touch of condescension, as in: We thought we were close back then, but look at what we've been through now, look at how the roots of our lives have entwined.

It seems that in life there is no gain that comes without loss. Surely one day I will think back on our son's infanthood with nostalgia, as well as his days as a young child, a boy, and then a young man. To live fully is to commit to things we are terrified to lose, all while knowing loss will come. It occurs to me that life is a series of deaths we must endure, and even somehow embrace, in order to let new life in. Maybe the same is true of our corporeal death, when our bodies will grow cold and lifeless. Maybe instead of fearing that day, I will try to take comfort in the model life has presented so far: New life sprouts in the spaces made by the losses we learn to endure.

―――――
――――

Something from Nothing

By Carol Paik

I had been thinking a lot about paper—specifically, about
how much of it I throw away and how wasteful that seems—
so I decided to try making some of my own. This happens to me from
time to time: I become overwhelmed with guilt about the garbage I
generate and I then think, well, it's kind of pathetic to just feel bad,
surely, there's something constructive that Can Be Done. At other
times when I have felt like this, I have taken up yogurt-making and
bread-making, not for health reasons or because I'm preservative-
phobic—quite the contrary, I'm all in favor of preservatives, at least
in moderation—but because it seems that yogurt containers, bread
bags, and paper are the three things I throw away in unconscionable
quantities and I have this vision in my head of the Pacific garbage
patch that won't dissipate. The vision won't dissipate, and apparently
neither will the garbage patch.

Making paper is actually fairly easy. (As it turns out, so is yogurt-
making, if you have a yogurt-maker, whose sole function is to control
temperature; and so is bread-making, if you own a bread machine. I
probably don't need to point out that purchasing these appliances,
compact as they are, negates the whole purpose of yogurt/bread/

paper–making, which was to reduce my carbon footprint. Also, they're only easy if you're content, as I am, with relatively pedestrian yogurt/bread/paper.) When I first read about papermaking, it sounded really hard. It sounded like it involved roaming around in the woods pulling up fibrous grasses and roots with gloved hands, pounding them with a wooden mallet or something equally unwieldy and full of splinters, or maybe stomping on them in a vat. It sounded laborious, in a tedious way but at the same time, in addition, as if it involved some mysterious technical dexterity, some sleight-of-hand. But really it's easy. And it does help if you buy Arnold Grummer's basic paper making kit, available online for about $30.95, which consists of a "pour deckle" (a rectangular wooden frame), "papermaking screen" (a piece of mesh), a sturdy plastic grid, a wooden bar, and a sponge.

And while you can certainly go out into the fields and gather plants and boil them and pound them and boil them again until the fibers lose their backbone and will, all you really need, and what the kit recommends, and the whole reason I wanted to make paper in the first place, is garbage. You take your paper garbage. You take your old copies of *Fitness* and *More (for Women Over 40)* magazines that you got free for running the *More* half-marathon last year and whose exhortations and promises now weary you; you take bank statements and credit card bills (from before you went paperless); letters from your kids' high school administrators about what they're doing to prevent sexual assault; requests for money from so very many worthy charitable ventures, so many that you couldn't possibly give to them all. In particular you take your drafts of the young adult novel you're no longer even remotely interested in finishing.

You take it all and you energetically tear it all up, first lengthwise and then crosswise, into jaggedy half-inch squares.

You put a few handfuls, or about as many scraps as could be puzzled into a letter-size sheet of paper, into a blender, add two cups of tap water and push "blend." The instructions say quite specifically that you should have a designated blender for this task. You shouldn't blend paper and then expect to use the same blender to blend your smoothies. Making paper is a toxic endeavor, as scrap paper is laden with chemicals. One papermaking book I read suggested going to the local Goodwill or the garbage dump and finding a used blender, but I would be afraid of something electrical that someone abandoned at the dump so I went to the hardware store instead and bought the cheapest blender I could find, although it was kind of hard to find one that didn't have fifteen different speeds. And of course that was frustrating, because the whole idea, remember, was *not* to buy another appliance! The whole idea was that I was going to be making something out of nothing, and making something out of nothing and reducing the Pacific garbage patch shouldn't involve purchasing a brand new blender. So already, before I even started, I felt a little defeated and sheepish.

But anyway, you take your non-fancy, non-European blender and blend the paper scraps and water, and when you have a blurry mess (takes about thirty seconds) you pour it into the wooden frame, which you have submerged in a small tub of water. There's a lot of sloshing of water involved in the papermaking process, so you have to put the tub of water in the kitchen sink. Many papermakers advocate making paper outdoors, but it was wintertime when I felt the need to make paper, so outdoors was not an option. It made me wonder, reading this advice, whether most people who make paper live in California, or Arizona, or some place idyllic and temperate, some place that isn't where I live, some place that doesn't have long, drawn-out miserable winters during which you sit indoors thinking about how your kids will be leaving for college soon and won't need you anymore and how you'd better come up with a new sense of purpose or at least some hobbies.

So you need to occupy the kitchen sink. If other people need to use the kitchen sink or the surrounding countertop area, this could pose a problem, especially given the toxic nature of what you are doing. But you don't care what anyone else needs right now, because you are determined to create something today, today you are going to make something, you are going to make something out of nothing, and that is a worthy goal, and one that is worth occupying the kitchen for, and if other people want to, say, cook, or get a glass of water, or something, they're just going to have to wait because you deliberately and considerately waited to do this until right after lunch after you'd cleaned up the dirty dishes, so that no one should really need this area for at least a few hours and it's not really asking that much for them to go away.

And furthermore those people don't need to hang around and silently and concernedly watch you blend scraps of garbage with water in a blender, either. They must have better things to do.

So, you can decide how uniform you want your pulp to be. You can blend it longer and have a very smooth pulp, or you can blend it less and have some identifiable bits of paper floating in it. This is one of the parts of papermaking that is up to you; this is one of the steps where you can express yourself. Making paper in a blender is not rote or mechanical. It is an art, and this is why: you can decide how long you want to push "blend."

Once you've poured the pulp into the frame, it floats around in the water and you dabble your fingers in it to distribute it around. Once the pulp seems fairly evenly distributed, you slowly lift the frame out of the water. There is a piece of wire screening across the bottom of the frame, and the pulp settles on top of this screen and as you lift it from the water a layer of pulp forms there. You hold it for a moment above the tub so the water can drain out, and then you are left with a layer of pulp that, once dry, will be your new sheet of paper.

The very first time I did this, it worked perfectly, and the second and third times, too. The pulp lay even and flat across the screen and I thought, there is nothing to this papermaking business. Not only have I tried something new, I have mastered it! In one afternoon! The fourth time I did it, however, with all the confidence of the seasoned, the pulp clumped up. I had to re-submerge the frame and stir the pulp around with my fingers several times until the screen was satisfactorily covered, but even then the layer of pulp was lumpy. I thought, good thing this didn't happen the first time, I would have given up right then. My initial taste of success was sufficient, however, to make me keep trying despite this setback—but when I kept stirring and lifting and the pulp still would not lie flat, I almost gave up anyway. Who wants to make paper? What a stupid thing to want to do. You can easily buy paper. It cost more to buy the kit and the blender than it does to buy like a ream of brand-new paper. What do I think I'm doing, saving the environment or something? Go through all this trouble, and for what? Take up this space, make this mess, spend this time and effort ... for what? For *whom*?

After this little paroxysm of self-doubt, I reminded myself that I am far too mature to have tantrums, that I am capable of handling a little frustration. I got a grip and went online. And the internet papermaking community rose to my aid.

I learned, through my research, that the problem could be that the little openings in the screen were getting blocked by paper pulp, making it so that the water did not drain out evenly. The screen needed to be cleaned with a brush. After I cleaned the screen, the pulp did in fact lie more smoothly.

Once you've lifted the sheet of proto-paper out of the water, you have to remove it from the frame. The screen is held in place by a plastic grid, which is strapped tightly to the frame with Velcro bands. You put the frame on an old cookie sheet (which you will never again use for cookies), unstick the Velcro, and lift the frame off the screen. And there is the paper, perfectly rectangular, with softly ragged edges that give it that unfakeable artisanal look. You then place a sheet of plastic over it and turn the whole thing over. You try to squeeze as much water out of it as you can with the wooden block, and when it's pretty well squeezed you sandwich it between two "couching sheets" (other pieces of paper).

Then the paper needs to dry. You press the new pieces of paper under a stack of books so that they dry flat. The drying is the only time-consuming part of the process. You have to wait overnight at least. After that you—or I, anyway—get impatient and leave the pieces out in the open to dry, and they end up drying curly even after all that time being pressed under books.

Once I get started making paper, it's hard to stop. You tear up paper, you pour in water, you push a button, you pour the pulp, you lift the frame, you remove the new sheet of paper. You do it again, if you want to. If you want to, you do it again. It can take on a rhythm. The grating noise of the blender no longer bothers you. You can become a little crazed. Soon there are damp couching sheets all over the kitchen. But tomorrow, you know, you'll have a satisfying stack of curly, bumpy paper to show for it.

The paper is not necessarily beautiful. Some of it looks a lot like dryer lint. Some of it looks a lot like garbage that's been ground up and flattened—surprising! But some sheets of paper are delicately colored from the inks in the recycled papers, and some have little remnants of words in them from the bits that you decided not to grind too fine. Some have truncated Chinese character limbs from the chopstick wrappers I used. Some have shiny bits from the linings of tea bags. One piece has colorful threads running through it that I harvested from the bottom of my sewing basket. Once you get the hang of it, you can start throwing pretty much anything in that blender. Even before you get the hang of it. You can throw almost anything in there, and you never know exactly how it will come out.

I've heard that all the molecules in our bodies have been used before. It's the same with the paper.

But papermaking isn't really transformative. You don't really make a beautiful thing out of ugly things. I was hoping that at least I was making a useful thing out of useless things, but that's not exactly true, either. I don't think I can use this paper to write on. I don't think I can run it through my printer. But still, I have a stack of paper where before I only had garbage. That feels like some cosmic gain.

When I decide I'm done for the day, mostly because other people do need to use the kitchen, I wonder what would happen if I had my own papermaking studio. With endless space and time to make as much paper as I wanted. To make whole, huge, luminous, empty sheets, using frames that require the entire stretch of both arms and all my upper-body strength to lift. Maybe I would make paper all day. I read about a man who does that, a professional paper artist. The Library of Congress insists upon using his papers to repair their most delicate treasures. But I wouldn't want to do that. I would get tired of it if I did it all day. I would hate the pressure I would feel from the Library of Congress to maintain my paper's quality. And what would I do with all that paper? The Library of Congress couldn't possibly want it all. It would accumulate in stacks, in various stages of dry and damp, it would rise in dense towers, my house would fall down, I would never be heard from again.

I learned in this process that paper is a relatively recent invention. It was only introduced to the Western world in the Middle Ages. I am trying to imagine a world without paper. What did people use to write on? There was vellum, which is not technically paper, as it is made from skins, not from the particular water-based process used for authentic paper. Mass-produced paper did not exist until fairly recent times. Before that time, how did people write? More importantly, how did they re-write? They couldn't, I bet. They probably couldn't have conceived of wasting precious writing materials on a shitty first draft. They would have had to know what they wanted to say, and they would have had to have been convinced that it was worth saying before they would even have thought of writing anything down.

I have a growing stack of my own paper now. Each sheet is crisp and substantial, like a very healthy kind of grayish cracker. I like to look at the sheets. Some of them are little collages in and of themselves, with random bits of color and texture that are visually and tactilely pleasing. But whatever beauty the paper possesses feels so accidental that I can't take any creative pride in it.

I shuffle my stack. I deem paper-making, overall, a qualified success, worth repeating when the issues of *More* start piling up. But in subsequent paper-making sessions I have been unable to recapture the thrill—no, I'm not overstating it!—the thrill, the magic, of seeing a perfectly flat, unique sheet of proto-paper emerge from the bath. Every sheet I make now feels like a product of a process, with some luck thrown in, rather than of magic. But maybe that's okay.

Red-Handed: On Shoplifting and Infertility

By Jennifer Maher

Resolve, The National Infertility Association of America, lists a variety of emotional and physical symptoms in response to not getting pregnant when you want to get pregnant. They include but are not limited to:

- Lack of energy (especially when you have an unsuccessful cycle, on medical appointment days, or when you will see a pregnant friend);
- Headaches
- Irritability (snapping at people or making mountains out of molehills)
- Insomnia
- Extreme sadness
- Inability to concentrate

Shoplifting is nowhere on this list.

Yet in the nearly three years it took me to conceive, along with over $22,000 in home-refinancing and credit card debt, I also acquired the following:

- One black large-ring pullback belt with double buckle
- A boxy caramel suede jacket with fringe on the front pockets and

hem
- Decadent Fig, Orchid Surrender, and Cheating Heart lipstick (Estee Lauder)
- Two bottles of 2006 Chalone Vineyard Pinot Noir
- The complete boxed set of *My So-Called-Life*

Much like infertility, shoplifting requires a certain kind of seat-of-your-pants creativity. Some seasoned lifters, for instance, line empty bags with aluminum foil to get past the door sensors; others rig bags with springs or wear enormous coats with hand-sewn secret pockets inside. Whatever the method of concealment, though, recreational shoplifting has long been considered an archetypal feminine vice, an impulsive pilfering of the phallus and the mirror image of castration anxiety. Secreting a skin cream in the feminine folds of your purse couldn't be more obvious in this respect. Or imagine a necklace up your coat-sleeve, its laminated price tag held fast like a nascent IUD. Think about the fact that just this year in a South Carolina outlet mall, they arrested a woman with over $1700 dollars' worth of stolen clothes in an empty infant car seat.

*   *   *

When I finally got caught, it was on the first floor. The first floor of most department stores is the sort of gateway drug of shoplifting because it is full-to-bursting with easily pocketed items such as makeup and jewelry, a whole range of objects no larger than an infant's palm or a deck of cards. I had just slipped a gold-plated chain necklace with purple lacquer beads into my shopping bag full of already purchased merchandise.

Standing in line to actually pay for something while you steal something else is a trick I thought I was clever enough to come up with on my own although, actually, it's quite commonplace. Cloaking oneself in the veneer of respectable consumerism has a certain logic: who would suspect someone who is in the middle of paying for something else? The calculations involved in such decisions (how much to spend, how much to steal) are both whimsical and precise, a weighing of the universe against your own held breath and courage. I was actually feeling sort of virtuous that day as I had passed up a display of patterned SmartWool socks, thinking somehow that a pair might be pushing my luck. Then I heard the voice behind me:

"Ma'am, you need to stop right now and come with me."

Of course I had no choice but to follow him, though he made me walk in front, somehow guiding my elbow without touching me at all. We rose up on the same escalator that, as a child, I used to be afraid would catch my shoelace and crush me. Resort-wear was on sale, and we passed turquoise and pink signs that read "Island Getaway" against a backdrop of pixilated palm trees and sand. I remembered then, oddly, that the first word I learned to read was "Island." "Is-land," I pronounced it (with an "s") to much praise, as I had I tried to sound it out and not just guess, which when it comes to words is just about as much right as wrong. I still cling to this skill—to be able to make a mistake and be redeemed for how I made it—even in the most awkward of circumstances. Perhaps if I just explained to this young man, I thought, as we rode past waffle grills and men's shirts and thick blue Mexican glassware, that this was all because I was thirty-seven years old and didn't have a baby. I had made a mistake but I could learn.

Yet I couldn't speak of these sorts of calculations as we turned right and left nearly a dozen times into the stained off-white recesses of the store, a place where doors no longer whooshed but were opened by punching a code into a metal box above a doorknob. This is where the logic of theft got you, I thought, as I was ordered to sit in a chair with leaky stuffing. This was the place for people like me, people who think the universe runs via a system of payback such that pilfered accessories could balance existential rage.

The gentleman who had caught me on a camera concealed in a mirrored pillar couldn't have been more than twenty-four years old, with dark hair cut close to his head. He called in a female sales assistant—store policy I later learned—and the only thing between me sitting up straight and passing out in fear was my ability to concentrate on her silver nametag and the garland of irises tattooed around her ankle.

Both of them were, I was sure, ridiculously fertile, with at least thirty years of potential baby making between them. She usually worked at the cosmetic counter where they wore white coats. By now I was so used to being administered to by people in white coats that I half-expected her to ask me the date of the first day of my last period and to take out a syringe of Lupron.

"Name?" he asked, as she rotated the ankle of her right leg in a circle and stared at her cuticles.

I learned that if I signed a paper saying that it was my first offense and I agreed to pay the store one hundred dollars and not shop there anymore (though I was allowed, he emphasized, to shop online whenever I wished), I could be let go without involving the police. It wasn't until he ripped the form off from the top of a pad of them that it really hit me that people did this all the time. I didn't know why anyone else did it. I only knew that for me it was a way of biding time and ferreting objects away until the empty space was filled. If I had been pregnant, I might call this magpie-like behavior nesting.

* * *

I saw a therapist for a while over my anxiety about not being able to get pregnant but not about my shoplifting; it seemed too personal. Her assurances that I had come from "a long line of women who were able to have children" didn't work for the obvious holes in its logic: anyone who has been born should therefore never suffer infertility. She prescribed me anxiety medication by consulting a laminated circular chart.

Years later, and after I finally had a baby, I learned that she had long been on a kind of informal shoplifting "watch list" at one of the more expensive boutiques in town. She hasn't been arrested for a number of reasons, I suppose, chief of which includes her being white, in her late sixties, recovering from throat cancer, and recently divorced from her husband of forty years who left her for his Japanese teaching assistant. (In a small college town information like this spreads quickly).

I imagine my therapist, even now, arms full of Academic Woman of a Certain Age clothing—long, flowing caftan-like tops with nubby printed textures connoting either travel or a degree in anthropology—clothes meant to encase their wearers like so much flocked wallpaper. When she hands over her Visa Gold she nicks a scarf, say, or a free-trade wallet whose earmarked profits benefit children in Guatemala with cleft palates. The clerks in the store keep a lookout and try to sense when she might take something in order to distract her, like shaking a bright plastic toy in the face of a crying infant. No one really has the guts to actually call her on it, and the store must make enough money from what she *does* buy that they can afford to leave her alone but for the watching. My reaction to this information is a combination of repulsion and sympathetic joy.

* * *

The fear of getting caught, as any therapist will tell you, is an endemic part of the thrill of shoplifting. The pounding of blood in the arms and neck, the panic-static in the eardrum, the bursting open of the department store's heavy glass and metal doors and into the air of the known world abruptly *accessorized* by what you both do and do not deserve. Thus the final steps out of the store are the scariest, and the most thrilling. I would draw this part out, lingering at the edge of tile and concrete, fingering the perfume bottles in an approximation of calm, my attempt to look less criminal and more casual consumer, a hassle-free flaneur with time on her hands and the world at her feet, a pantomime of the person I wanted to be. Not a thirty-seven-year-old academic whose left hip was covered with raisin-sized bruises from hormone injections. Just a woman. A woman shopping, as women do, for something warm and soft.

* * *

Of course, the stealing only quelled my pregnancy obsession for short periods of time. I still zealously counted the days of my cycle, took my temperature and recorded it in shaky print on a series of post-it notes next to the bed, bought package after package of ovulation kits and debated on the toilet seat whether the cervical mucus stretched between my fingers was, in fact, an inch or more in length, and if the opening to my cervix felt like more like my lips or my nose (the former connoted the approach of ovulation, or was it the latter?). For three years I would periodically sneak my index finger into my underwear to check for blood as the twenty-eighth day approached, the absence of which would mean I could breathe for the next hour. When my period came, as it inevitably did, the pelvic tugging and the thick molasses cramps became yet one more sign of the fact that the more I wanted something, the less likely I would be to get it, that I couldn't count on getting what I wanted without subterfuge. Once stopped at a red light (probably on day twenty-six or twenty-seven), I reached up under my skirt with my left hand only to see the man in the SUV next to me raise his eyebrows and smile. You'd think that such embarrassment would warrant something good later to make up for it, but still that month my period came. Later, standing in line buying tampons, I palmed a tin of mints the size of a swallow's egg.

* * *

Statistics vary, but most agree that women are born with a finite number of eggs, somewhere between one and two million. Approximately 750 eggs are "lost" each month and even fertility specialists throw around the term "shelf-life" to refer to the ways in which a woman's eggs begin to diminish in quality after her twenties. One doctor called it the "dried macaroni problem." If you have a box of dried macaroni on your shelf, you can expect it to last for years and years. However, the longer it sits inside your dusty cupboard the more likely it is that when you set it to boil, some of the individual pieces will have deteriorated.

* * *

I have never stolen a box of macaroni.

* * *

Part of what makes shoplifting seem alluring is also that you can pretend that you are striking a blow against the facts, against a world where the age you are able to pay your bills and live without three other people splitting the rent is also the age at which your peak fertility begins its precipitous drop. Stealing then felt to me like a swipe against Mother Nature and Father Capitalism at the same time. After all, that sweater at the Gap? It was made by fertile women at maquiladoras being paid cents a day.

*   *   *

Across the parking lot from my pediatrician's office is a large department store whose red star signals its function as a space of gratification, both imaginary and concrete. When I carried my son into and out to of my car for his first checkup, I was afraid someone would stop me. I love him so much that I'm still not convinced he will disappear into thin air for everything I have ever done.

*   *   *

Two weeks ago, I saw my old therapist on the front steps of our local organic grocery store. It was October, and she had just tucked her cell phone into her wool pocket after calling (I imagine) for someone to come and collect her. By the time I was finished shopping, I saw her get into a taxi and leave the store's order behind, turning her back on shelves, radio frequency identification tags, video cameras, prices for objects per can and box and gram and ounce. Before she stepped into the cab, her long linen skirt brushed against a pile of pumpkins arranged by the entrance, their round ridged orange skin fairly glowing in the shadow blue of early evening. They were still sitting there as she drove away. Right out front. Anyone could have taken one.

Shelving My American Dream

By Dina Strasser

"You know what I'm going to do when I grow up, Mommy?"

This is a frequent topic of driving conversation between my ten-year-old daughter and me. The acoustics kind of suck in our car, but when we talk about this particular thing, I never pretend to hear what I haven't heard clearly. I lean my head backwards between the seats and turn my ear towards my daughter, without taking my eyes off the road.

"I'm going to start a bakery named Blue Sky Bakery. I will serve pie and gumbo. Do you need to go to college to start a bakery?" she asks.

"It depends," I say, smiling. "A two-year college can get you some good training in food prep. But you can also go to a fancier school, like the Culinary Institute in New York City, or Le Cordon Bleu in Paris." I've looked this up. I'm feeling virtuous for already supporting my daughter's edgy entrepreneurial pie-gumbo fusion career path.

You can do whatever you want, I say.

And then I stop. My jaws click shut, belatedly, on the lie.

*   *   *

In June of this year, I turned down the most prestigious scholarship for doctoral work that my local, nationally recognized university had to offer. It was as generous as you could hope for: full tuition, opportunities for stipends and grants. The gracious professors there, and others who helped me with my applications, spent hours of their own time walking me through the process, writing recommendations; they said, to wit, you were born to be a Ph.D. And I knew it, because I had figured that out for myself in third grade. It was the only lifelong dream I have ever had.

My husband had always, warmly and unequivocally, supported me in pursuing the doctorate. Yet we now had a fairly unusual set of circumstances to consider. He: a Presbyterian minister, where work was increasingly hard to find, poorly paid, and mostly located in the South and Midwest. My only brother: mentally disabled. My mother: widowed. And me: needing exquisite mobility to find the kind of rapidly dwindling tenure-track job required to support my family, most of which were located in places best described as not in the South or Midwest.

It wasn't adding up. But we tried. We spent three solid weeks, after we knew the amount of the scholarship award, talking to absolutely everyone: friends and family in academia, professors, ministers, finance people, each other. We looked up stats on line, took notes.

Finally, we went to a local diner for breakfast. I brought steno pads. We spent four hours there, the waitress stoically filling our coffee cups over and over as the "Pro" list filled one side of one page of the pads, and the "Con," six sides. The decision was obvious. I made it.

I spent the next few days befuddled. I wrote apologetic, heart-broken notes, in a fog. Someone had not died; something absolutely had died. I had not lost anything; I had lost everything. I spun like a top on the pinpoint of an invalid assumption: that culture and commerce will part like the Red Sea in the face of your training, your commitment, your talent and desire.

Had I not, like any privileged, educated, self-aware person, identified my bliss? Had I not found and assiduously practiced what I was born for? Had I not fulfilled my obligation to Henry David Thoreau and Joseph Campbell, to step firmly away from the life of quiet desperation, to find and nurture the thing that makes me come alive? Where was the world meeting me half-way? Where, goddammit, was my reward?

"What do you want to do when you grow up?" asked the third grade teacher, and I said, "I want a Ph.D. I want to be an English professor."

"Why do you want one?"

Because I loved to read and write, and I wanted to teach other people to read and write and to keep reading and writing myself. This was my castle, under which I had thought I had built all the right foundations.

Nearly thirty-five years later, I heard Mike Rowe of *Dirty Jobs* fame in a TED Talk, quoting a farmer he'd met. "Following my dreams," the farmer said, "was the worst advice anyone could have given me."

* * *

My grip on the dream had loosened by the time my husband and I decided to have kids—but only to the degree that I felt I could not physically have children safely by the time I finished a doctorate part-time, as our financial situation then dictated. I counted myself lucky to know the statistics in that regard, thinking of my brother, and the steep, cold slope between the chances of having a kid with Down's in your earlier versus later decades of life.

So kids came first. My priorities were asserting themselves, so nascent as to be practically dripping with afterbirth of their own.

I didn't see the grace in this at the time, although I wanted children very much. It was only what I needed to do, somewhat grumpily, without the power to simultaneously exist in two different dimensions. I want two lives, I would think to myself. Or three, or four.

You can do anything you want, only not at the same time, said a friend to me around that time. I don't remember who it was, but in my mind, it was one of my most talented and ambitious soul sisters, and I was blessed to have plenty of them. Magazine editors, advocacy lawyers, dancers. The foment of their lovely lives seemed to lend even more gravitas to the words.

I latched onto this phrase and put it on like water wings. I repeated it to myself with every pang of intellectual hunger. I would do this thing, the thing I was born to do. Someday.

* * *

So what has been the result of my decision to say no to the Ph.D.? To stay in a related job that pays double the national average with good benefits, in a decent school district, with marriage and family healthy and happy, in a big blue colonial that houses a fridge, pantry, and medicine cabinet that, by all rights, I should just empty into a cardboard box and mail to Haiti. I should mail the whole house to Haiti. This is not Sophie's Choice.

And yet I ended up asking around anyway about our culture's obsession with the dream come true. I nose through books and articles because if I know one thing, I know how to find the answers to life's deepest questions: research.

My mother is a genealogist, so I asked her what American generation she felt would be most akin to our own: where we looked toward a life for our children that would be demonstrably worse than the one we experienced. "There's always the Great Depression. But there was also one during The Panic of 1819," she wrote to me in an email.

The what?

It was the first peacetime financial crisis of the nation. "Your ancestor George Wells got stuck administering his father-in-law Meshack Hull's estate in New Jersey from about 1816 on, for years," mom writes. "In 1829, he was actually jailed for being for debt, though he'd been very prosperous before. His wife and children, instead of being able to stay on the family farm, had to leave the county and, in the case of his son, find another kind of work. George disappeared around this time, and it is assumed that he died, whether by his own hand, or naturally, being a question in my mind."

I also asked my good friend Mary, who has her own doctorate in

American history. She has routinely served in the role of perspective-giver in my life: when I was battling through post-partum depression over the deeply non-crunchy-granola C-section birth of my daughter in 2003, she was the one who gently reminded me that in 1803, the baby and I both probably would have died. (Priorities.)

She felt that our closest parallel was the 1970s. "The country was gripped in an economic recession, manufacturing jobs were starting to disappear, the country seemed to be going to hell in a hand basket—Watergate, Vietnam, Iran," she said. "One thing that historians point to is the number of disaster movies in the seventies. American exceptionalism started to crack."

Which was interesting. Three historical periods, all different, of wondering how to suck up hardship and hand it to your child. Maybe through disaster films. *World War Z*, anyone?

I assumed that the American Dream came out of generations actually achieving, to some degree, the American Dream—and no one can deny the general upward trend of the standard of living. But maybe a single life, a sixty-year span if we're lucky, is not enough to really detect that slow crawl to civil rights and antibiotics.

Could it be that there is a reverse dynamic at work: The American Dream, as panacea for the many, many times—the majority of times?—that dreams did not come true?

Mary and I also talked, at length, about the Ph.D.

She told me that she believed that every doctoral candidate has at least one Stupid Reason for Getting a Ph.D. "Mine was to show the world that I am smart," said my wise friend. "Why do you want one?"

And I realized that my Stupid Reason for Getting a Ph.D. ran as follows: "To not be lonely."

And one more truth comes clear, one more layer of scale scrubbed from the eyes.

*   *   *

Something will work out, my mother would say to me after yet another agonized Ph.D. indecision-fest on the phone.

It's a deeply kind catchphrase. It's better than the first two I tried. But it's not enough. It's only the place where your sequined tutu, your fictitious blue bakery, your unearned doctorate, is honored by people who love you, and who know better than to make you a promise.

*   *   *

I have enough contact with the upper echelons of academia that at times I am still and suddenly wracked with envy. I'll hear of some lecture, some conference. Discussing Hume as the sun sets seems then to be akin to paradise lost—because that is, of course, is how all doctorates spend their time. This scenario also involves French cheese.

These flashes are decreasing, though. It's as if the decision actually worked, in one more reversal, to help me not to long for a misplaced future, or a misspent past, but simply, be in the present. I am, in the main, happy there.

Happy, but not content. For I still don't know how to handle the bliss question with my kids, and that seems to be of paramount importance—especially now, when I'm reasonably certain that at least climate change is going to make many more big decisions for my children than it ever (never) did for me.

When my daughter lays plans for her gumbo from the backseat, or my son chatters about being selected for The Voice, what loving parental slogan do I use? What alternative vision do I weave for my children, in the face of the seductive, beautiful, barren American dream? And how do I do this without crushing their own creativity, their sense of the possible?

It's not *you can do anything you want.* And it's not *you can do everything you want, just not at the same time.* It's not even *something will work out.* There's a step, a saying beyond this, something at which my fledgling Buddhist practice is trying to aim, maybe. But I'm not sure which slogan fits it best.

There may be no slogan for the control of life's outcomes. And we do love slogans, this side of the Atlantic. No wonder America has no words for it.

*   *   *

"Why do you want one?"

The last time someone asked me why I wanted a Ph.D., I answered in that way that happens sometimes, when a truth comes out of your mouth without any premeditation. I was older than eight, and I had dropped some of the bullshit—maybe I was ready to articulate the bottom line.

"Because I want to know something that deeply," I said.

The friend who asked, having begun his own doctoral work that year, nodded in approval, and I felt as if I had passed some kind of test.

But I sense that the real deep knowledge—the real test—is now.

I remember the moments after making the decision finally to let go, looking at that mound of steno pad pages, pushing my cold eggs around my plate.

It felt very strongly like the night when my husband asked me to marry him, twenty years ago— the start, really, of the chain of events that had led me here.

That night, I did not scream in delight, or cry in joy, although I did a lot of that later. I wasn't even aware, at first, of really feeling anything at all. I was, instead, waiting.

I waited for fear, for resistance, for alarms to sound, doubt to flood in, for my usual inner voices to clang and chime.

Instead, everything went still: as still as a pond before you drop in a pebble, and step back to watch what happens.

───────
═══════
───────

Fear

By William Bradley

Fear of fire, fear of lightning, fear of fire caused by lightning, fear of falling trees, and of those people who drive their cars into houses or gas stations because they confuse the brake with the gas. Once on Central Park West a man reached for my wrist as he said, "Can I ask you something?" but I didn't let him. Fear of unasked questions that will never be answered. Fear of Rumpty-Dudget a character in a book, 'Rumpty Dudget's Tower,' that I have never read, but whose worn blue spine I can sense on the bookshelf in my parents' living room at all times, even now. Fear of women in high heels; fear of Mrs. Stein, my second grade teacher; fear of other people's carelessness. Fear of small but deceptively sharp knives, like the Swiss Army knife that cut my brother's finger so deep only one of my mother's maxi-pads, with wings, could hold the blood. Fear of sirens, though only when I am driving and cannot tell where they are coming from; fear of North Korea; fear of visiting Turkey, where I was born, and not being allowed to leave. Fear that there is something really really wrong. Fear that there is nothing that can fix it.

—A. Papatya Bucak, "I Cannot Explain My Fear"

My wife and I each paid twenty dollars to attend the one-night-only twenty-fifth anniversary screening of the original *A Nightmare on Elm Street* several years ago. This was at a point in our marriage where we probably couldn't afford to blow forty dollars on a movie, but I had just started my first academic job and, for the first time, we had an annual household income of over $25,000, so we felt rich. More importantly, I love *A Nightmare on Elm Street* and was excited for the opportunity to see it on the big screen.

If you asked me for my favorite horror movie, I would honestly tell you that it's *The Shining*. Kubrick's use of tracking shots, Bela Bartok's score, Shelly Duvall's performance as an abused woman trying to survive in an icy, opulent hell—it's all amazing and remains unnerving every time I watch it. But if I have a few beers tonight and decide I want to watch a scary movie, I'll probably put something like *Friday the 13th Part 3* in the DVD player. You can watch it in 3D in the comfort of your own home, you know. But more importantly, I find that cheesy slasher movies from the seventies and eighties just have their own sort of goofy charm. Yes, they're violent, and more than a little misogynist. But it's so hard for me to take them seriously at this point. Even though they were rated R, they seem, in their simple-minded black-and-white morality, childish to me. Not of the morally complicated adult world I live in, that's for sure. So watching movies like these reminds me of my childhood, keeps me tethered to the dorky, horror-obsessed kid I was, and—I sometimes like to imagine—keeps me young.

*   *   *

Even before I saw my first horror movie, I found them fascinating. When I was a kid, my parents were diligent in shielding us from movie gore and anything remotely scary; the idea, I know, was to protect our impressionable minds from anything that might upset or disturb us, but I'm afraid it didn't entirely work. In fact, as I got closer to my middle school years and realized that most of my friends had seen *Halloween* and *Silent Night, Deadly Night*, I became acutely aware that my parents had been sheltering me: there was a whole world of supernaturally-powerful serial killers and blood-thirsty demons out there. And though I understood, rationally, that these things only existed in movies, on some level I think I perceived something menacing about the adult world as a result of my parents' zealous protection. After all, if there were nothing to really be afraid of, then why would I need to be protected?

But maybe that's not quite right. Maybe my brother and I detected menace before becoming aware of these movies, and that's what caused my parents to try to shield us from multiplex mayhem. I know that the witch in the *Wizard of Oz* scared me when I was a kid; so too did Dr. Banner's transformation into The Incredible Hulk on TV. And my brother couldn't stand to be in the room when *The Electric Company* started—the voice that yelled "Hey You Guys!" would cause him to cry if he heard it. And, truth be told, he was well into adulthood before he could force himself to watch the scene in *Indiana Jones and the Temple of Doom* where the villain rips the guy's heart out of his chest. So, perhaps my parents—realizing that their sons were high-strung and easily frightened—understood that they had to be on their toes when it came to shielding us from big-screen frights.

Or, maybe I'm over-thinking the whole thing, and responsible parents just don't let their kids watch R-rated movies full of naked breasts and chainsaw-wielding madmen who want to turn teenagers into barbecue sandwiches.

The bottom line is, by the time I was in the fifth grade, most of my friends had seen at least some of these movies, and I had not. I was fascinated by the very idea of these forbidden movies, what they said about the adult world, and why my parents felt the need to shield me even while my friends' parents did not feel a similar need to shield them. Plus, there was that nagging suspicion—then, as adolescence was just on the horizon—that there was something more than a little lame about not knowing anything about these movies that were so important to my classmates. I was already beginning to understand that I was a dork—a label that would stay with me at least through the beginning of high school—and part of that dorkiness came, I understood, from my naïveté when it came to these elements of the popular culture that were so important to kids in the eighties.

I found my entrance into this world of horror that my friends knew so well one morning in the cafeteria before the first bell rang to send us to our classrooms. A kid I knew, Jeremy, had a book in front of him—*The Nightmares on Elm Street*, the official novelization of the first three Freddy Krueger movies. The films' logo—which looked like it had been scribbled by a madman with a nerve disorder—was splashed across the cover, with Freddy's razor-fingered glove hanging down, blades partially obscuring the title with the blood that dripped from them.

In all of my eleven years, I had never seen a book that looked so cool.

"Good book?" I asked him.

He nodded. "Yeah. The movies are better, though."

Of course they were, I thought. "Why are you reading the book then?"

He shrugged. "I just really liked the movies." I think he must have intuited my interest, because he said, "I'm almost done with it. I'll bring it tomorrow, if you want to borrow it."

Jackpot. Jeremy had allowed me to find a loophole in my parents' "No Horror Movie" rule. They didn't make R-rated books, after all—and weren't my parents always on my case about reading anyway? Even if they found the book, I could always use their previously articulated arguments in favor of literacy against them. Finally, I had won. I would learn exactly what was so scary that my parents had felt the need to protect me.

I felt certain that reading the *Nightmare on Elm Street* book would allow me a deeper understanding of the real world.

* * *

I didn't just read the book—I devoured it like a Romero zombie devours brains.

As I read it, I realized that books, too, could be scary. I had an imagination vivid enough to picture what it must have been like for Rod to see Tina's sleeping body rudely lifted from the bed by an invisible force, shoved to the ceiling, and split open by unseen razor fingers. I could see Tina running from Freddy, his arms somehow long enough to stretch across the entire alley, affording her no escape. I could imagine Jesse's dread as he came to realize that Freddy intended to possess his body in order to kill in the waking world.

The irony is, I probably would have been better off watching the movies, as far as my own fear went. When I finally saw the movies, I did find them scary, but I also realized that Rod and Tina were obnoxious and older than they should have been—they spoke the way people in their thirties think teenagers speak ("I woke up with a hard-on that had your name on it." "Tina's a four-letter word—your joint's not big enough for four letters."). The scene where Freddy chases Tina down the alley looked so fake that it made me giggle when I finally saw it for the first time. And Jesse was just an irritating whiner—if Freddy wants him so badly, let him have him, I'd later say.

But that's not how I responded to the novelizations. No, the novelizations were simply terrifying, and—since Freddy Krueger killed kids in their sleep—I promptly resolved to never sleep again.

I didn't actually make the decision consciously, of course. I may have had an overactive imagination and very little idea about how the real world worked, but I wasn't an absolute moron. I knew, logically, that child murderers do not come back from the dead to haunt the dreams of the children whose parents burned them alive in their own boiler rooms. It just didn't happen—and if it had, it would have been all over the news. No, if people could come back from the dead and hang out in people's dreams, I was fairly certain that my grandfather would have checked in from time to time. The premise of the movies was not grounded in reality—it all came from this guy, Wes Craven, who wrote and directed the first movie. And, I could convince myself during the day, that guy probably lived in a mansion in Hollywood, surrounded by movie stars and supermodels, and hardly ever thought about this creation of his that was haunting me so.

That was my rational mind. But how many perfectly rational eleven-year-olds do you know—particularly when they're in a dark room and the rest of the family is asleep and the house is making weird noises?

My parents realized pretty quickly that I seemed groggier than usual at breakfast, and that I was falling asleep while watching TV in the afternoon. And I eventually had to tell them that I wasn't sleeping much at night anymore, and why. I can't say my parents were angry with me, but nor were they particularly pleased. When all is said and done, I think the situation kind of annoyed them. "You're not sleeping because you're afraid that a boogeyman in a fedora hat that you read about in the adaptation to a movie you've never seen is going to kill you?" I don't think that's the type of question any father wants to ask his son.

As stupid as they surely found the situation, I have to say that my parents bent over backwards to help me to sleep again. No more drifting off in the afternoons. A big glass of warm milk before bed. God love them, at one point they even took me to our family doctor, apparently hoping that there was a pill or something that would make me forget to be such a neurotic coward. The doctor, for his part, seemed confused about what his role in this personal drama was supposed to be. "I would say," he eventually concluded, "he needs to get over it and start sleeping again."

Which is exactly what happened. As time passed, my terror over what I'd read faded. In a few weeks, it all seemed silly, and I was quite embarrassed by the whole episode. Scared by a movie character? How dumb. I promised myself that I would never mistake supernatural fiction for reality ever again.

I kept that promise, too. For several months. Until the USA Network showed *Children of the Corn* one afternoon when I was home sick, and the process repeated itself. Just as it would a year or so later when I saw *Halloween* for the first time. And then again with *Friday the 13th*. These movies terrified me as a kid, but I couldn't stay away from them.

As an adult, it's a rare and special thing to find a horror movie that's genuinely scary. *The Shining, The Exorcist,* and *Alien* still retain the ability to unnerve, and I'll occasionally find an older movie, like Bob Clark's original *Black Christmas,* that really freaks me out. But too much of what passes for horror these days seems watered-down, or too outlandishly stupid to be taken seriously, or just not scary. I can't imagine anyone watching the recent *A Nightmare on Elm Street* remake and actually getting frightened.

Of course, part of the problem is, I've found new things to be scared of. As it happens, my parents were shielding me from the menacing adult world; it was just the nature of the menace that I'd misunderstood. There are no doll serial killers or leather fetishist demons with pins in their heads—instead, there are religious extremists with bombs. There are factories dumping carcinogens into streams. There are people who think a life devoted to literature and art is simply decadent. There's waterboarding.

I fear that my writing is mediocre at best. I fear that my wife no longer finds me as physically attractive as she used to. I fear that I'll never realize my dream of becoming a tenured professor. I fear impotence. School shootings. Stand your ground laws. Getting drunk and revealing how offensive and obnoxious my internal monologue actually is. Cancer. Being revealed as the academic and artistic fraud I'm pretty sure I am. That my parents will die. That my wife will decide she no longer loves me.

These are the things that terrify me. Sometimes, the only way to calm my nerves and quell the fear is to turn my brain off and watch a madman with a butcher's knife stalk and then kill some babysitters.

* * *

The twenty-fifth anniversary screening of *A Nightmare on Elm Street* was kind of a bust, actually. I had this idea that the theater would be filled with aging Gen-Xers excited to recapture the experience of being a child of the 1980s again. And there were a few of us like that in the audience. But there was also a group of about fifteen teenagers sitting down in front, and they were pretty rowdy—shouting things at the screen, giggling, running around the theater, making and receiving phone calls. My shushing got louder as the movie went on; a woman roughly my age sitting nearby eventually shouted at the kids, "Shut the fuck up!"

"This is ridiculous," I kept whispering to my wife.

"Do you want to go complain?" was her constant reply.

I didn't. I didn't want to be the type of person who gets annoyed with young people. I didn't want to be someone who gets angry at the sound of teenagers laughing. I hated the idea that I was the type of grumpy old man who said things like "Get off my lawn!" or who had groups of teenagers thrown out of places because of shenanigans and tomfoolery.

Towards the end of the movie, as Nancy is setting her traps for Freddy, one of the teenage girls came walking up the aisle, gabbing into her phone.

"Oh I know," she said, "it's soooooo stupid, but funny..."

As she walked past me, I leaned towards the aisle and shushed her as loud as I could.

She stopped and adjusted the phone so that it wasn't near her mouth. I was expecting her to whisper "Sorry," but instead she looked right at me and shouted, "Shut up!"

I was shocked, startled both by her viciousness and the phrase that entered my head immediately: "My God, I would never have spoken that way to an adult when I was her age."

When I was her age. Back in the day. The good old days? The grownups I knew when I was a kid didn't think so—they thought we were out of control, with crack cocaine, gangs, drive-by shootings, casual sex, and N.W.A. Of course, their parents thought they were out of control, with their LSD, free love, campus protests, left-wing radicals, and The Beatles.

Unexpectedly, I did experience fear that night—the fear that comes from knowing that, somewhere along the line, you became old without realizing it, and you'll never know the reckless energy of youth again.

———————
———

The Pageant

By Shaun Stallings Anzaldua

Ahh, the Pageant. My family's greatest Christmas tradition was the product of my mother's desperate struggle against in-laws for the rights to Christmas Eve. When the Pageant was born, twenty-five years ago, my brother Larkin and I were my mother's only adult children who lived close enough for her to realistically expect to see us every Christmas. We both married into families with strong cultural and religious customs surrounding the holidays. Our new families always gathered Christmas Eve for tamales, empanadas, presents, and church. Both of our in-laws are Catholic, the divas of ritual and tradition. On Christmas Eve they attended midnight mass, complete with incense and holy water. Our own Christmas Eve traditions had been less predictable. We were raised Quakers, so we had no midnight mass of our own. Some years we crashed the service at one of the local churches; some years we didn't. Most years my mother would try to coax us into singing Christmas carols, but once we became teenagers, Christmas Eve involved spiked eggnog and going out more than family togetherness. Not that my mother ever gave up trying. All in all, our family customs most certainly lacked the strength and conviction of our spouses.'

For the first several years of our marriages, Larkin and I tried to squeeze my mother into our holiday plans, but we rarely made it to her house on Christmas Eve to sing carols or drink hot cider. She was struggling against the bond between our spouses and their families, their mothers in particular. It was like pitting Elmer's School Glue against Gorilla Glue, an unfair contest by any measure. However, my mother is the little bulldozer that could. She is, as she will often say, a problem solver. She wanted to ensure that we would feel the same inexorable pull to her at the holidays that our spouses felt towards their mothers. She understood that what she needed was a compelling event that could carry the weight of Mary in a manger, holding dear baby Jesus, five pounds, six ounces, wrapped in a swaddling cloth.

And so, the Pageant. It was the story of the Nativity, to be performed on the evening before Christmas Eve. It started off small. Just the family, a few bathrobes and ties around our heads for the shepherds, a nightgown and shawl for Mary, and a plastic gold crown for King Hared. And scripts. My mother had written scripts for each of us. But overall the production was quick, simple, no room at the inn, star rises in the east, Mary has a baby, sing a few carols, and it's done.

The second year, my mother wanted to add depth and earnestness to the evening.

"Wouldn't it be great if each of us brought a gift for Jesus?" she said enthusiastically. "Just like the wise men!

"I could tell a story! Larkin could play a song on his guitar!" she continued with truly disturbing glee. She was blind to the looks of horror on all of our faces.

My sister-in-law once removed (I believe that's the technical term for the sister of a sister-in-law) was sixteen and a cheerleader at the time.

"Jen, how about you bring a cheer for baby Jesus?" my mother asked.

At sixteen, Jen did not yet have the wisdom or perspective see the golden opportunity in front of her. My beloved Never-Here-at-Christmas-Because-He-Lives-in-Los-Angeles brother Josh, when told this story many years later, immediately rose to the occasion that Jen had passed over.

"Give me an 'N'! Give me an 'A'! Give me an 'I'! Give me an 'L'! Give me an 'S'! What's that spell? NAILS!!'" Josh cheered as he flung himself against the wall in the shape of a crucifix. Josh is decidedly *not* Christian. My Catholic middle school–aged daughters nearly wet their pants at this, and instantly decided Uncle Josh was the coolest person they'd ever known. The nuns at their school were less taken with the cheer when the girls performed it for their friends at school after the holiday break.

But Jen was just a teenager at the time and could only roll her eyes and say, "Ah, yeah. Great. I'll get right on that Mrs. Stallings."

I wish I could say that we entered into this yearly production willingly, lovingly, and with true holiday spirit. The truth is there was much rolling of eyes from all of us and whispers of how bossy my mother can be. But despite our resistance, she never gave up and, in fact, her zeal and resolve seemed to grow with every passing year. So while there were no cheers for baby Jesus, we did put on the robes and the ties around our heads and said our lines with as much sincerity as we could muster. We siblings do like to amuse ourselves however, so we lightened our load by adding in lines like "And Mary rode Joseph's ass all the way to Bethlehem," and "We three kings of orient are, smoking on a loaded cigar." My mother was too immersed in her role as director and producer to notice.

Over time the production became more and more elaborate. We invited friends, especially ones we could sucker into playing parts. We added real costumes with tunics and headpieces, feathered angel wings, sound effects (God on a boom box), and even a balloon star that did indeed rise … from behind the piano.

One year, ashamed of my bad attitude and failure to see the beauty in this humble play, I promised myself that my gift to my mother would be to surrender to the season and enter into the event with true love and kindness. I was doing well until we had to take a trip to the costume shop to buy new shepherd's staffs and donkey masks and, for goodness sake, a new crown for Hared. The first store didn't have good shepherd's crooks and frankly their crowns looked cheap. We needed to go to the costume store on the *other* side of town. It was the height of the Christmas shopping season and traffic was snarled. Every station on the radio was playing stale Christmas carols sung by barking dogs. I desperately wanted to abandon the quest, but my mother was high on Pageant crack, and nothing was going to stop her.

I tried. I really tried. But I reached my limit, forgot my promised gift and screamed like a nasty teenager. "It's a fucking pageant! A pageant we do in the fucking entry way of my house!" So much for true love and kindness.

My mother ignored my bad mood and on to the costume store we went.

As our children grew, much of the Pageant burden shifted to them. They advanced from sheep and donkeys to speaking parts. Heaven help the granddaughter foolish enough to bring home a boyfriend to play in our reindeer games because she was sure to be cast as Mary and her bewildered boyfriend as Joseph. Nothing cements a fragile adolescent romance like having to play an unwed pregnant teenager and her new baby daddy in front of an audience.

When the children were little, they looked forward to the Pageant and entered into it with joy. They were serious and studied their parts and had to be sure their costumes were just right. Then the grandchildren invariably hit an age where the only way to get them to participate was to say through clenched teeth, "Do you want to break Grandma Jane's heart? Do you? Do you want to be the one to ruin Christmas?" Later they go would off to college and begin to miss the symbols of childhood, and return, ready to mock and make snarky remarks with the rest of us. The year my mother turned eighty, we took the Pageant on the road and performed it in a little community center in the rural California town where my mother had moved. We graduated beyond the entryway of my house to a theater with a real stage. Her birthday guests never knew what hit them.

The Pageant successfully fulfilled my mother's purpose. For over two decades, she had a night all her own: a night that transcended Christmas Eve. She took it on like a Broadway pro. Each year she lovingly brought out and ironed the costumes, fluffed up the angel wings, and replaced the crooks that had been turned into swords or chewed by the dogs. She reviewed the scripts and assigned the parts and looked forward to an evening surrounded by family.

My mother is eighty-three this year, and travelling from California to Texas has become harder for her. For the last two years, she has lived in a retirement community where she has made a lovely circle of friends. This year, she told us she would not be coming at Christmas, and could we please send the costumes and scripts out to her. She has a whole new cast to direct, a group that will likely do much less eye rolling and complaining under their breath. I like to think of her and her elderly friends dressed as angels and shepherds and sheep. I wish I could be there to hear the lucky woman who gets to speak Mary's line about never having been with a man. In spite of my pettiness, the Pageant has come to mean Christmas to me. It has been a constant in my children's lives. Some years annoying, other years joyful, but always there. A thread that bound my family to my mother, year after year. I thought it was forever, just as I would like to believe my mother is forever.

Maybe this year I'll try to guilt my teenagers into wearing bathrobes and scarves. I am not the powerhouse that my mother is, but it's worth a try. I think I won't ask them to make up any cheers. At least not this year.

Under the Bed and Dreaming at Hillside House

By Jennifer James

About thirteen years ago, my husband's grandmother, Miss Elizabeth, was moved to an assisted care facility. Initially, it seemed surprisingly nifty. There were big screen televisions, prepared meals, and lots of friendly staff members. Except for the occasional funky smell and confused outburst, it felt a lot like a geriatric college dormitory setting. This was a happy surprise—I had anticipated grungy green walls, stained linoleum floors, and rows of abandoned bodies anchored to wheelchairs. Instead, I walked into an open, airy atrium, decorated with large, luxurious Boston ferns and a spacious bird cage, home to a few brightly colored finches. Two cheerful ladies sporting tight perms and meticulously coordinated track suits greeted me as I stopped to look more closely at the finches. I was not crippled by sadness, walking into this place: a genuine blessing under the circumstances.

All kinds of folks landed at Hillside House, as I'll call the facility. Elizabeth had been diagnosed with some nasty "female" (it was, in fact, uterine) cancer six months earlier. She had most likely been ill for some time before the cancer had been detected, but she had ignored some symptoms, assisted by well-intentioned physicians along the way. By the time her illness was acknowledged and diagnosed, it was statistically unlikely that Elizabeth would recover. Her treatment plan was labeled "palliative," designed to give maximum comfort and healing without subjecting her to rigorous procedures and quasi-lethal medications. Reluctantly, the family agreed that she could no longer live independently and Hillside House seemed the least-terrible option available. Which didn't make it any less terrible for Elizabeth.

* * *

When I first met Elizabeth, she was in her late fifties and I was engaged to her grandson, Ed. Ed and I had met in college, fallen quickly and completely in love, and caused our parents all kinds of consternation as a result. Especially Ed's parents. My parents were divorced and disorganized and fairly unconcerned with societal expectations and judgments. Sure, they hoped Ed was not secretly a serial killer with a collection of severed Barbie doll heads under his bed, but he seemed respectable enough, with his gentle Southern accent and aspirations to become a high school English teacher. On the scale of crazy in our family, he was hardly a blip on the screen.

Ed had grown up in a small, rural community, where your life was fodder for community review sessions, courtesy of your friends, neighbors, and your very own respectable family members. What they knew was this: I had not been raised in Virginia, my (ahem... divorced) parents were both Yankees, and I had been baptized in the Catholic (aka "Papist") church. I could have come with more familiar credentials, and certainly, a more civilized bloodline.

Still, Ed seemed to like me fine, and that was good enough for Elizabeth: she fed me right along with the rest of the family. Ed grew up three miles down the road from his grandparents and spent many happy days eating freshly fried chicken and as many ice cream sandwiches as he could manage at their kitchen table. Elizabeth didn't talk about how she felt, or how you felt, or what was wrong with the world today; she was busy putting more potatoes on your plate and checking to see if you needed more chicken. She was a pragmatist, by necessity—dreamers in her time didn't have a great survival rate. After all, there was too much work to do: there were parents, and grandparents, and if you were very, very lucky, children, to care for. Elizabeth did what was expected of her: she tucked her own dreams away and nurtured those of her children.

And Elizabeth loved children. She taught them handwriting and prayers and how to slaughter a chicken neatly. She fried piles and piles of salt fish and potatoes at four-thirty a.m. on winter mornings so "the boys" (she'd had two, three counting her husband) would have a good breakfast before they set out hunting. Both of her sons married spirited women who may have wanted their husbands home on chilly winter mornings, and as the years passed, Elizabeth found herself preparing fewer and fewer early-morning fish feasts.

When I came to the family, Elizabeth and I developed a heartfelt, if timid, affection for one another. We didn't really speak one another's language, but eventually I learned to shift my conversation to weather predictions and local news, and she learned that I was not judging her on the tenderness of her chicken or the tartness of her fig preserves. We became allies in the muddy world of multi-generational family allegiances, and by the time Elizabeth became a resident of Hillside House, she was much more like my own grandmother than any kind of in-law.

About three months before Elizabeth got sick enough for anyone to notice, I learned I was pregnant with my first child. This was a considerable relief to everyone involved. Initially, our families feared that our lickety-split trip to the altar indicated that a "six month" baby was on the way. After a year, there was no baby. Several years passed, in fact, with no baby, and family members began to wonder whether we were incapable of reproducing or just too selfish. Ed and I kind of wondered ourselves, so when we learned a wee one was on the way, we leaned into the future with happy resignation and notified our parents and grandparents accordingly. The ensuing excitement was tinged with achy sorrow as Elizabeth's illness unfolded parallel to my pregnancy.

*   *   *

So there we were: Elizabeth, wondering how she'd ended up in this silly establishment full of old people and food without nearly enough seasoning, and me, wondering kind of the same thing.

One afternoon, as we sat in a sunny spot on the back terrace, a tiny, hunched-over woman who I'll call Miss Emily shuffled by. As she went back in, she threw us an accusing look, as if we'd just pelted her car with raw eggs or something like that.

"What's wrong with *her*?" I asked. "Are we sitting at her table?"

Elizabeth snorted, coughing a little in the process. "Aw, don't worry about her. She's always on a tear."

"Why?"

"I don't rightly know, honey. She won't talk to anybody. She just rushes around here like somebody's after her." Elizabeth sipped her chamomile tea. "It sure is aggravating, I'll tell you that."

I saw her point.

*   *   *

A few weeks later, Hillside House had become much more familiar to me. It felt less like a college dormitory, and more like the set for an episode of *The Twilight Zone*. At first, everything had seemed pretty normal. Which I guess it was, since aging and death are normal realities. Still, it's outside the norm to find a whole building purposed for housing folks in this chapter of life, and there was a certain sensibility that colored the residents and their visitors accordingly.

For example, we'd gotten used to a woman I'll call Miss Agnes, who sat on the loveseat in the corner, singing, "I'm ready, I'm ready, I'm ready for my ice cream." Sometimes she got a little pissed and sang louder, in a growly tenor: "I'm READY. READY. READY FOR ICE CREAM." And so on. The nursing assistants spoke to Miss Agnes gently, and would sometimes guide her to the next activity or simply let her chant the day away, dreaming of ice cream.

One afternoon, Miss Emily skittered by the periphery of the room we were sitting in, and I asked Elizabeth if she had heard anything that might account for Miss Emily's strange behavior

"Oh, honey," Elizabeth sighed. "Miss Emily is nuttier than one of Grandma Sutton's date bars." That much I knew.

This was her story:

Miss Emily was a book thief. Since her first day at Hillside House, she'd been collecting printed materials. She started with a stash of brochures at the front desk and soon moved on to the large print *Reader's Digest* magazines. Because she only took a few at a time, nobody noticed at first. God knows, no one ever saw the woman sitting, much less settled in with a good book. Two or three weeks into her residency, however, Miss Emily's secret was uncovered. The staff tried to keep the old lady relatively happy, while quietly culling her print collection from time to time.

I was impressed. I wasn't sure I'd be innovative enough to snatch reading materials like that.

Elizabeth let out a very soft *harrumph* and said, "Well, Jenny, I don't know what in the world that crazy old woman is thinking. What is she going to do with all those foolish books anyway?" I said nothing in response, but thought I knew exactly what "that crazy old woman" was thinking. Exactly. And I tried not to hold it against Elizabeth.

* * *

Books are not a nicety for me; they're a necessity. Books have always been my friends. There were long periods of time in my childhood when I was surrounded by lots of unhappy adults and books and not much else. The books made excellent allies, even the duller ones. Also, since the adults involved were pretty busy being miserable, they didn't have too much energy to squander policing my reading selections. I learned a lot about sex (a few choice scenes from Peter Benchley and Ken Follett) and frontier living (Laura Ingalls Wilder) and deeply disturbed loners (Edgar Allen Poe) at a tender age.

As I grew older, and mercifully, gained access to a broader selection of books, I glommed onto young adult fiction. At a certain point in time, I probably could have recited full chapters of Judy Blume books from memory. I loved a book called *The Cat Ate My Gymsuit* by Paula Danziger. I am still moved to tears by Madeleine L'Engle's *A Ring of Endless Light*. The clueless (if loving and well-intentioned) adults in my life had very few helpful pointers for a chunky teen with poor social skills. If Judy Blume couldn't teach me how to talk to boys, who could? Who *would*?

In the end, if you're a reader, it doesn't seem to matter so very much *what* you read. There is magic in seeing the world from another point of view, regardless of whose it is. And yet, there are some people who never quite get the magic. Elizabeth was one of those people. She read when obligated, but reading held no special pleasure for her. Maybe it correlates with the "no dreaming" environment she survived; her life had been shoved into external experience. Reading was an activity only the idle could afford, and she was too busy making sure that everyone was equipped with clean undies to read some trifling book. And hell, who really knows what batty Miss Emily was up to? Maybe she was just an elderly hoarder. She never said.

I like to think she read everything she took, though. Especially the *Reader's Digest*. When it's me, sitting in the determinedly cheerful atrium of Hillside House or Young at Heart, or wherever I end up in my final days, I hope I'll have books to read, and I hope they'll be my books, and not crappy little fliers and magazines stashed around the assisted care facility. I can see the fun in skittering around and snatching things too, though. It doesn't matter if you call it a nursing home or an "assisted care facility" or the geezer house. What it means is, you can't live by yourself anymore. Because you're too old or too sick. And the next benchmark is not a new car or Hawaiian vacation. Even the crazy lady singing for ice cream had to know that. So you might as well enjoy the ice cream and read everything you can.

*   *   *

I never did talk to Miss Emily, and Elizabeth lived for ten whole days after our baby was born. On the way home from the hospital, we stopped by Hillside House to introduce our new boy to Elizabeth. It was quite an event. Elizabeth was very sick by then, and spent her days drifting in and out of awareness.

Ed and I walked into the familiar atrium with the baby, hope and despair in equal measure bubbling around in our hearts. The old ladies gathered around to coo at the little one and to give us hugs. I was sobbing before we even got to Elizabeth's room. The rush of raw joy and sadness coexisting made everything seem so terribly fragile.

We walked into her room. One of her sons sat beside her bed, holding her hand and quietly weeping. My husband and I sat down on the other side of the bed and she shifted her head slightly so she could see us.

"Oh, Jenny," she said softly. "He's just darlin'." Then she managed a wink and a tiny chuckle. "Little boys are the best, you know."

She was too weak to actually take the baby in her arms for long, but I put his tiny body down in the crook of her arm and he stayed like that for a minute or two. Then the spell broke and the baby cried and we had to leave.

We saw her one more time after that and the baby cried from the first moment we walked in. Finally, someone took the baby into another room, and Elizabeth took my hand.

"Jenny. Jenny, do you think I'm dying? Do you?"

In general, I like to think I'm okay being near very ill people. I think it's because I am gifted in the finest nuances of denial and can carry on a quasi-normal conversation with the dying. I can discuss the weather, their medication, other family members, etc., etc. The problem is, I don't want to scare the dying person. If *they* don't know they're dying, I don't want to be the one to break the news.

I took a deep breath. "I don't know. I think that's between you and God, Elizabeth. I don't know. But either way, it'll be okay."

Elizabeth coughed slightly and squeezed my hand. "I expect you're right, Jenny. I expect you're right."

Just then, my husband walked in and reached for Elizabeth's hand, resting his on top of mine. "Grandma, we're going to have a little boy running around our hill again." My chest caved in. She would never see our little boy run down the lovely, green hill that lay behind our house. It was the same hill she'd run down as a tiny girl, and that her children, and her grandchildren had called home. I thought I might smack my husband in the gut for reminding her of what would never be.

Of course, Ed was just as frightened as Elizabeth was, probably more so. And all he could imagine was how much she'd enjoy feeding another little blonde boy with an enormous appetite and smiling eyes. I think he was so happy and proud to have our little dumpling of a person to show his grandma that for a moment, he forgot that the story would go unfinished for her.

Elizabeth smiled again, the perfect grandma, wanting to comfort one of her boys one last time.

"Oh, Eddie," she said softly. "I'll dream of it."

Proxy Sister

By Karrie Higgins

As a gentile living in Salt Lake City, the holy beating heart of the Church of Jesus Christ of Latter-day Saints, I probably have no right to meddle in Mormon religious matters, even though the Church meddles in secular ones every day: a prohibition on Powerball tickets, a ban on adoptions by cohabitating couples, arcane liquor laws that turn restaurants and taverns into temperance-era time machines, Proposition 8. I certainly had no right to attempt to claim a place in the standby line for the Priesthood Session of the LDS October 2013 General Conference. Besides being a gentile, I am also a woman: strike two. In the Mormon faith, men get the priesthood and women get motherhood. Men bestow blessings and women birth babies.

Strike three: I am childless.

Strike four: childless by choice.

After four years in Utah, during which I had learned to soften my loudmouth and dodge conversations about family and children, it astonished me when Mormon feminist organization Ordain Women called out the Church on its separate-but-equal lie: Motherhood is not equal to the priesthood. Motherhood is equal to fatherhood. Only priesthood is equal to priesthood.

Until Ordain Women made headlines, I was only dimly aware of Mormon feminism. I had heard of excommunicated feminist scholars and a "wear pants to church" protest, but Ordain Women felt more direct and radical, more relevant.

Ordain Women believes the priesthood should transcend gender and parenthood, just as Joseph Smith intended in 1842 when he envisioned the Nauvoo Female Relief Society as a "Kingdom of Priests." Without the priesthood, women cannot take the reins of clerical or ritual authority. Men oversee everything they do, even in the all-female Relief Society. When the Church limits women's roles because of motherhood, it echoes patriarchal justifications for locking women out of everything from the voting booth to education.

Maybe if women held the priesthood keys, I thought, they would spring open doors for me, too. Maybe I could finally claim a place for myself here, a childless gentile in Zion. Do not get me wrong. Everywhere I have lived, I have endured relentless uninvited commentary about my choice not to bear children. I am *selfish*. I am *depriving my parents of grandchildren*. I will *never know real love*. I will *never be a true adult*. But here in Zion, the commentary cuts deeper: Here, I am *denying spirit babies their bodies*. Here, I am defying God's commandment to "be fruitful, multiply"—and risking the salvation of my soul. I am *going against God's plan*. The patriarchy of the church trickles down into my life, too. What happens to Mormon women happens to me.

So on October 5, 2013, when Ordain Women attempted to claim places in line for standby tickets to the priesthood session, I joined them although I did not join them as myself. I joined them as a woman I'll call Sarah, who could not attend and whose name I drew from a stack of proxy cards, similar to the LDS ritual of getting baptized by proxy for a deceased ancestor. I was her proxy sister, and it was my sacred duty to carry her to the door of the Tabernacle.

At least, that was my justification on that day. Now I know I had it backwards: she was the one who carried me.

*   *   *

Hours before walking to City Creek Park where Ordain Women gathered for a prayer and hymn, I realized I did not own a stitch of appropriate attire. Every member of Ordain Women, I was certain, would show up in raiment befitting potential priesthood holders. All I had was a closet full of hippie patchwork dresses, boyfriend jeans, and Chuck Taylor All Stars. On the one hand, patchwork dresses are at least *dresses*; on the other, you can see the silhouette of my thighs when sunlight hits the diaphanous cotton gauze—not exactly modest attire for Temple Square. Gentile that I am, I still respect the sacred space beyond those fifteen-foot walls. Plus, it was chilly, the first true autumn day. As for the boyfriend jeans: modest but sloppy. Tomboyish.

Too broke to justify new clothes, I was trapped in a double bind: dress like a boy or stay home.

Would my baggy jeans insult these women who yearned for the priesthood so badly they were willing to risk apostasy—or worse, excommunication? Would I attract hecklers? Then I realized that my dilemma represented the secular vs. spiritual tug-of-war I face every day living in Salt Lake City: How do I navigate Zion's spiritual and cultural expectations of femininity and modesty while staying true to who I am?

I *had* to go.

On my way to City Creek Park, I stopped in Temple Square and listened to Elder D. Todd Christofferson's voice booming almost God-like over loudspeakers.

A woman's moral influence is no more or nowhere more powerfully felt, or more beneficially employed, than in the home.

I found myself transported to the first time I heard words thundering over a loudspeaker. It was a union picket, probably 1979 or 1980. I was four or five. A man chanted, "Solidarity Forever," and picketers sang back, a call-and-response. I never forgot it, the visceral feeling of words at that volume, how they vibrated in my heart and bones. As Elder Christofferson spoke, I watched a pair of little girls, maybe six years old, spinning in frilly white flower-girl dresses by the edge of the reflecting pool, as if rehearsing their future wedding dance. *Most sacred is a woman's role in the creation of life.* Were these their first loudspeaker words, the first ones to vibrate inside their hearts?

The world has enough women who are tough; we need women who are tender. There are enough women who are coarse; we need women who are kind. There are enough women who are rude; we need women who are refined. We have enough women of fame and fortune; we need more women of faith. We have enough greed; we need more goodness. We have enough vanity; we need more virtue. We have enough popularity; we need more purity.

Families picnicked on the lawn east of the looming temple spires: men with their suit jackets strewn on the grass, sleeves rolled up, backs of their hands shielding eyes from the afternoon sun; women tossing napkins and sushi trays into Harmon's grocery store bags, wiping their toddlers' mouths.

Nobody reacted.

If this were Portland, Oregon, where I lived for nine years before moving here, somebody would have raised a fist and shouted. *We have enough patriarchy! We need less theocracy!*

I was an ex-pat in my own country. And yet, part of me must have assimilated. Why wasn't I raising my fist? Why wasn't I shouting?

As I stood up—

Take particular care that your dress reflects modesty, not vanity, and that your conduct manifests purity, not promiscuity.

—I thought again of the hippie patchwork in my closet and felt good for choosing my comparatively modest jeans.

Then, as if to put me in my place, a young elder walked by, looked me up and down, and scowled. I could almost hear what he was thinking: *Tomboy. Dress like a woman.*

* * *

By the time it was almost my turn to approach the Tabernacle door, I already knew it would not turn out the way that Matthew: 7 booming over the loudspeakers in Temple Square a few hours earlier had promised: *knock, and it shall be opened unto you*. Not this door, not this time. The guard standing sentry at the bottom of the steps had turned away Ordain Women founder Kate Kelly, and the news trickled down within minutes to the rest of us, along with a message to stay in line: each of us would knock at that metaphorical door, even knowing the answer. We would force the Church to cast us out one by one, not just our gender, but *us*.

Up until the moment she was turned away, Kate Kelly had believed—really believed—the door would open for her. What for her had been an act of pure hope and faith had for the rest of us transformed into a ritual drama.

Earlier, as we walked two-by-two from City Creek Park to Temple Square, we passed elders holding up signs, the best-dressed beggars I have ever seen in their starched white shirts and black wool suits.

"Need Tickets," their signs read.

Nobody around me seemed to notice this reversal of the normal order in Zion: men beseeching women. I thought the elders meant it tongue-in-cheek, a jab at Ordain Women for attempting to "steal" their tickets.

Then, after we arrived at Temple Square and stood shivering in the early autumn chill, I noticed an elder clutching a sign to his heart:

"Be an answer to prayer. Need tickets."

I knew then that the elders on the sidewalk had been sincere, and in fact, their signs were not directed at us at all. Walking past the conference center, we simply happened into their path.

By contrast, Ordain Women rules forbade begging tickets off sympathetic male friends or relatives. This protest was not about *getting in*. It was about *being let in*. Still, I wondered why we did not thrust signs into the air and chant. Did the elders milling about on the square know why we were there? Did the frilly princess girls? How could they know our purpose if we did not assert ourselves in some way?

A sister missionary wearing a star-print dress in Wonder Woman blue-and-white and a red corduroy coat passed by, arm hooked in her companion's. Her nametag bore a United States flag. Her outfit, I realized, made her the embodiment of that flag: a living, breathing Lady Liberty. If this were a protest in Portland, I could safely interpret that dress as a "statement." Here, though, I am still learning how to read. But my questions cut deeper, too. As a man had asked me just before the group left City Creek Park, "How do you do a religious protest?"

Until Ordain Women, all my protests had been secular.

I once dressed in all black for a theatrical funeral procession through downtown Portland to protest the Carabinieri shooting Carlo Giuliani at the Genoa G8 Summit in 2001. At the front of the march, several "pallbearers" carried a black cardboard coffin aloft, which we planned to lay at the door of the World Trade Center. On our way there, we staged a die-in in front of the *Oregonian* newspaper offices.

Another time I locked arms with a line of strangers to prevent donors from exiting a parking garage to attend a fundraising dinner for President George W. Bush.

In Seattle, I chanted, "This is what Democracy looks like!" and "Whose streets? Our streets!"

In Washington, D.C., I plopped down in resignation on the lawn in front of the World Bank as riot police circled our demonstration.

Locked arms, blocked intersections, costumes, signs, chants, dances, drummers, direct actions, handkerchiefs shielding nose and mouth in case of pepper spray: these signify protest to me. But how do you mount a religious protest, where your target is a higher authority?

And in Zion, is there ever really a difference? In March 2011, I attended a protest in the Capitol Rotunda against a bill that threatened to strike at the heart of Utah's model public records access law, the Government Records Access and Management Act. Conservatives and liberals joined forces, and for the first time since moving here in 2009, I felt like I could claim a place in this community. As I ascended Capitol Hill on foot that day despite an aching knee and a fever, I realized how hungry I had been to get involved in civic activism again, to carve out a space for myself as a Utah citizen. I moved to Utah kicking and screaming when my husband landed a promotion he could not refuse, and for the first few years, I barricaded local politics out of my life, refusing to learn representative names or follow the issues. As a liberal gentile, I felt like I had no voice, anyway—no hope of being represented. Even most Democrats in this state sound like Republicans to me.

Inside the capitol, I was shocked at the politeness of the protest. Protestors held signs—

Talk About a Freight Train

Sunshine Not Secrecy

GRAMA may be old, but she has a voice

Only Cockroaches are Afraid of the Light

—but they did not, as Portland anarchists would have, lock arms and shut down the capitol. They spoke their minds for the appointed time and dispersed on cue.

What made the protest culture here so polite? Was it just the conservatism of the state in general or something about the Mormon culture? Then, someone said, "You know the Church is behind this bill. If you're fighting government secrecy, you're fighting the Church."

In other words, there is no such thing as a purely secular protest in Zion.

But is there such thing as a purely religious one?

Now, standing in line at the Tabernacle, I clutched my proxy card, worried if I loosened my grip it would float away on a breeze. Back at City Creek Park, when organizers had invited attendees to carry proxy cards, I knew I wanted to do it. I felt the desire viscerally, a physical ache in my lungs. It was so intense I almost reached for my inhaler until I realized this ache was not asthma: it was a testimony, Mormon-speak for burning in the bosom, the fire of truth.

I wondered what it meant to volunteer to get cast out for somebody else—and for somebody else to request it. It was the opposite of a proxy baptism, when living Mormons stand in for the dead, getting dunked in the baptismal font on their behalf, a magical telegraph bouncing from star to star: *you are wanted in our fold*. My proxy was alive, inhabiting a body, and she had telegraphed me through her

Mormon sisters.

What if these women knew about the afternoons I spent circum-navigating their temple during my early days in Salt Lake City, longing to tap into that magical telegraph machine and zap a signal to my dead brothers in the phantom zone? Or the time I wrote my brothers' names on a slip of paper and carried it to the temple doors, where for just a moment, I considered sticking it into the lock like a pathetic skeleton key?

Was I so desperate to tap into the temple telegraph machine that I was using Sarah to do it?

On the loudspeaker, Elder Christofferson had derided feminists for scorning the "mommy track," but he was wrong. Back at City Creek Park, I had witnessed an Ordain Women member fielding urgent texts from her daughter about an eleventh-hour homecoming dress catastrophe. All around me in line, women fussed with strollers and tended to toddlers. And just as I had predicted when I scorned my baggy jeans in my bathroom mirror, the Ordain Women members came dressed worthy of the priesthood: most of all Kate Kelly in a mustard yellow, waffle-knit blazer and purple pencil skirt. These women radiated color, a stark contrast to the elders' black-and-white suits. Even here, I did not fit in, except for this: All my life, people like Elder Christofferson have assumed I thumbed my nose at mother-hood, but they never ask why I do not want children, just like they do not ask these women why they want the priesthood.

Ask, and you shall receive.

Suddenly, it felt right for me to carry Sarah to the door of the Tabernacle. Who better than the gentile, the childless-by-choice tom-boy in boyfriend jeans, to be cast out on her behalf? For that is what I am, always, as long as I live in Salt Lake City: an outcast. Marked, set apart.

One by one, women ahead of me approached the Tabernacle steps.

One by one, they sought entrance.

One by one, they were told, "Entrance to this event is for men only. Please go to LDS.org."

The guard meant they could log onto LDS.org to watch the priest-hood session live for the first time in history, the perfect Orwellian maneuver: nobody could accuse the Church of sexism if women could live stream the priesthood session at home—*at home*, there was that phrase again. *At home*: where I had almost stayed because of a stupid outfit.

When it was my turn to break from the line and approach the Tabernacle alone, I glanced from the crowd of people to the men snap-ping camera shutters at the front of the line and thought, "Nobody knows I am doing this as a proxy." Should I announce it? Was it dis-honest to let them think I was Mormon? Or could they already tell?

I looked up at the temple. How did I not notice before? Our ritual was playing out in the shadow of the west central tower, the one with the Big Dipper carved into it: the constellation for lost souls. In the basement below lies the baptismal font, where proxies stand in for the dead. If the temple really were a telegraph machine, the tip of that Big Dipper handle would be the wire connecting to the sky, to Polaris, the North Star. From there, any soul can be found, maybe even living ones. Maybe my proxy sister's. Maybe by standing here, I was trans-mitting a message to her.

I swallowed hard: dry tonsils, pill-stuck-in-my-throat feeling. "I am seeking entrance for me and"—I thrust out the card instead of speak-ing her name, as if exorcising her from my body. I needed the guard to see her as separate from me.

To my surprise, he leaned forward and read her name. He did not hurry. As a Mormon, he understood what it meant to be a proxy for someone. He understood I was carrying a burden. In this small act, I had transferred my burden to him.

But I had given myself away all the same: No Mormon in the bap-tismal font would exorcise her proxy. I was a phony.

The guard looked me in the eye. "Welcome to Temple Square," he said. "Entrance to this event is for men only."

For the first time, I felt the full weight and power of the Church bearing down on me, as if for that moment, the temple had been tilted from its foundations just a crack to let me peer inside at the baptismal font, then dropped, Wizard-of-Oz like, crushing me. It did not matter if I thrust out the card. What mattered was my heart. I had become her. I had become a Mormon woman.

I maintained eye contact as I nodded.

I did not cry because I did not know if Sarah would cry.

Finally, I understood: This protest was not a protest at all, but a prayer. We did not need signs because Heavenly Father could read our hearts. We did not need chants or locked arms or sit-ins because in the very submission the Church demanded from us as women, we held the trump card: We had made them tell each and every one of us no. We had made them witness our submission. We had made our burden theirs. It was not a ritual drama; it was real.

As I rejoined the crowd, a brilliant green dump truck loaded with trash bags barricaded us from the door: picnic detritus of the day— paper cups, sticky silverware, empty sushi trays, greasy napkins—the very things the Church's strict gender divisions define as "women's work," were now a literal barrier to entering the Priesthood Session.

The women, however, did not decry their fate. Instead, they broke into a hymn: "I Am a Child of God."

I was the only one not singing, the only one who did not know the words.

*   *   *

In an intersection on our way back to City Creek Park, a man dressed in a devil costume with a University of Utah Utes hat pointed a pitchfork at us and growled, "It's just like Hair Club for Men. You can't have it because it's for men!"

Was he mounting a secular protest or a religious one? After all, in the Mormon faith, there is such a thing as false testimony, a burning in the bosom inspired by the devil instead of Heavenly Father. And yet, that Utes hat: a cheeky reference to the annual "Holy War" between the BYU and Utah Utes football teams. I got the sense the Dark Lord of the Hair Club for Men was more riled about women's social roles than any doctrinal dispute.

But then, isn't that what we had just protested: social roles *as* doctrine?

Behind me, a man shouted, "Satan is a Utes fan? Oh, come on!"

*   *   *

Later, when we returned our cards so our proxy sisters could keep a tangible memento, I asked if I could contact the woman on my card. I wanted to tell her how it felt and what it meant to me to do that for her. The organizers suggested I write my name and email address on the back of the card, so I did. Even if she never contacts me, we are eternally connected as proxy sisters now, our relationship sealed by that artifact, an unofficial temple ordinance record.

On my way out of the park, I asked one of the women if it might offend my proxy sister to have a gentile carry her name to the Tabernacle.

"Non-LDS men can attend the priesthood session," she said, shrugging. "Why not you?"

I knew right away what she meant: If non-LDS males who possess no other credentials for the priesthood than their gender can attend the priesthood session, certainly non-LDS women who live under this patriarchy can, too.

But for me, it also meant something more fundamental, something less and something more at the same time: *Why not me?*

———
———

Hope Floating

By Robin Schoenthaler

I was forty, and single, and pregnant, and jubilant. I blossomed during a perfect pregnancy and then proceeded to give birth to a beautiful baby boy I named Ryan Peter Schoenthaler, eight pounds twelve ounces and twenty-one gorgeous inches long. He died nine days later in my arms, still and cool.

I buried that boy on a sunny hillside in a tiny casket designed to look like a bassinet, and by the time I stumbled out of the cemetery, I was a dead woman walking. Some days I couldn't keep my eyes open; other days I could barely speak. I dreamed in adjectives: *impossible, unbearable, unimaginable*; I woke up with verbs: *pulverized, imploding, eviscerated*.

Two years later, I gave birth to a boy named Kenzie James. I got through the pregnancy and birth through denial, plain and simple, with one permanent price tag: nine months of total amnesia. Of that period of pregnant pause, I remember OJ Simpson and I remember grinding my teeth, and that is really all.

Three miscarriages and three years later, when my last son came along—Cooper Craig Schoenthaler—I was wholly awake and fully attentive and I remember everything. Of the six pregnancies, I am left with one birth story.

Cooper was delivered by Cesarean section. An average C-section takes six or seven minutes from incision to delivery; Kenzie's took an endless half-an-hour; Cooper, eleven minutes. Eleven minutes to a lifetime.

I lay there while they opened me up again, floating along the arc-line that had gradually and irrevocably led me to this scene—lying flat on my back in a yellow room with bright lights. I was a woman physician under the care of women who started out just like me, women who struggled over books and tests and money and hostile men in positions of power for years at a time and who now put their bodies and souls on the line.

I remember my obstetrician Sharon coming to my hospital room at midnight to attend Ryan's brain-dead baptism. I picture her holding my hand in the NICU that night and then again and again over the next five years. I think of all the phone calls: I would sob and she would let me make any appointment any time as I worked through the surviving of survivorship.

I think of all the tables I have laid on and all the doctors I have seen—a long line, a stately procession—giving me good news and bad news and no news at all. I think of Ryan's delivery and his death. I think of how I lifted his body straight up above me, offering him to the sky. I think of Sharon two years later holding Kenzie aloft, in triumph, a giddy elevation of child-spirit, a peak moment, a crystal. I think of the dim light in Ryan's NICU room where his soul sailed away, and the bright lights in Kenzie's delivery room when his soul sailed in.

I think of the night light that Kenzie uses—how at three he is already such a singular little person who wants to look at books alone at night, how his soul is full of light and always has been. I feel the presence of both Kenzie and Ryan very distinctly within me, as well as a whole line of women who have given birth before me—my grandmothers and my friends, my mom and all the bereaved women in books and on buses.

I listen to the heartbeat monitors and think of Ryan's heartbeat ceasing and Kenzie's frantic heartbeat when he's feverish and the roaring in my ears each time I miscarried and I can't help but compare them to the steady beat-beat-beat that is my own heart's rhythm in this room at this moment.

It's a long eleven minutes.

Then I hear Sharon start to croon. In seemingly an instant, she again holds one of my sons aloft in the light. The overhead lamps create an aura, a halo, an embrace and I experience blindness reversed as the light heightens every pore and every limb and Cooper is outlined in beauty, screaming shrieking bloody beauty. He is alive, he is aquiver, he is a soul.

They bring him to me wrapped up and warm. I get my first good hard look at him: he is red-faced and dumbstruck, and I am the same.

I reach for him. No one says a word. The room is quiet; it feels like an altar. There's no heart monitor machines now, no barking loudspeakers, just the murmuring of Sharon and her partner, and the nurses counting sponges. I kiss Coop over and over—his perfect cheeks, perfect skin, perfect neck. He turns to me when I speak.

I lay there with this miracle in my arms, flooded with all that can happen over the course of half a decade. I remember the long period after Ryan's death when a pain-free interval seemed impossible, when anguish never ended and never waxed or waned.

But I realize, lying there, that somehow, somewhere, something carried me through. It is too strong to call it "hope": there was no hoping back then. It's too strong to say it was anchored in me—it was not. But it must have floated, in and out, with the moon, or with the seasons, or maybe with each breath.

Because something helped me hear the muffled words that sometimes bounced off the sheer rock cliffs of my pain. I began to hear the voices in the cemeteries I visited—voices of mothers who murmured that if I could just keep breathing long enough the tunneled darkness might begin to lift. I began to see the anguish of my cancer patients in terms of cells defying death. I began to connect myself to a humanity bound up with suffering—plague victims, war dead, road kill, religious martyrs, and most of all a long line of women who had keened over children in caskets.

Something had taken hold of me. It wasn't optimism or confidence or faith in an equitable universe—that was gone and would never come back.

It was much fainter: a tiny turning, a whispered murmur, a miniature red berry lying deep and dormant. But the berry dropped a seed and the seedling took. A tiny bud appeared and on it there must have been a drop of dew, and that was where I let that little thing that must have been hope float. I never touched it, I never named it, I really never even knew it was there. I just let it float. I let my hope float. I let my hope float on an impossibly tiny bud and now I had another son, I had two more sons.

They move us to the recovery room where it is dimly lit and quiet. Cooper nurses. I am pain-free and at a level of peace that is hard to describe to this world. I curl up on the gurney in the darkened recovery room, all dreamy sated senses.

Eventually the nurse and I begin to chat. She remembers Ryan well. "Every time I pass Room 428 I think of all the flowers you left behind," she tells me. Then we coo about Cooper, how beautiful he is and already such a good nurser and so alert and connected and smart.

She tells me then about her own difficulties with conceiving, her doubts and how frightened she has become. I can so completely relate to this young woman at the beginnings of yet another long trail. She says to me, "We've tried so hard to have a baby, but I'm afraid to keep trying. How did you keep your hope alive?"

I start to tell her, but I hesitate. I'm suddenly tired beyond imagining, my eyes and limbs feel weak and I am nearly asleep. I murmur, "Just let it float." She says, "Hope Floats? Isn't that a movie?" and I giggle into the pillow.

Lying there laughing, I feel them like a flash flood, the raw and precious lives that led us here: the lives where pain has a beginning but anguish has an end, where seasons start and berries fall, where there are voices that can pierce the darkness and where cells that split can mean life in one year and death in the next and where there are webs that connect us with our ancestors and that in the darkest winter there are buds that can act as cradles and that hope may not spring eternal but that it can absolutely float.

———

Someone Stole Home

By Antonia Malchik

Great Northern Bar in Whitefish, Montana, had once been a real local hangout until it got into all the guidebooks described as "a real local hangout." Now, the round, garrulous bartender serves too-clean tourists alongside locals with greasy baseball caps and drooping, walrus-sized mustaches.

Over pints of Moose Drool we've been chewing over local development, which has been moving at an accelerated rate since the Aspen Corporation bought Big Mountain, the ski hill under which Whitefish is clumped.

The brown ale's malty flavor makes me wonder what took me so long to come back home. When I left my hometown first for college and then to live overseas, I didn't know if I would permanently return. As a travel writer, I lived happily in Europe, Russia, and Australia, keeping the static image of my perfect home with its clear mountain air as an assuring beacon. Montana, I assured myself during my twenties, was my last best place. It would always be there.

That was until I took my English-born husband Ian to Whitefish and reality socked me. We're looking to move back here, Ian and I told the bartender, but the property prices are staggering. "Where are all the young families goin'?"

"Eh, C-Falls, Kal'spell," he figures, wiping down the counter. Columbia Falls and Kalispell, Whitefish's neighbors, have always been more blue-collar than my hometown, where former hippies nurtured a nature-loving tourist industry.

"You don't sound like you're from here."

"I'm from Tennessee."

"Beautiful country."

"Yup." A slosh of the rag sends my empty glass skittering and he gets me a refill. "This is a better place though. Or useda be. I bin here twenty-five years. It's not the same."

"You think the town's dying?" He puts cash in the register and shouts at a white-haired tourist who's brought his loafers and khaki shorts too far behind the bar.

"It's already dead."

* * *

At our bed-and-breakfast's rustic log tables, Ian and I fall into chatting over huckleberry waffles with a couple from Texas. Our first morning, we got talking real estate, where I voiced shock at the rise in property prices (more than double since my mother sold her house five years before) and our worry that we wouldn't be able to afford moving back. Now, in some sort of self-flagellation, I can't stop talking with them about their plans to buy a vacation home here.

The man has a slightly chagrined look as, with defensive smugness softened by a Texas drawl, he says, "I guess we're part of the problem." This friendly, tidy, golf-playing guy and his wife then relate their previous day's real estate search, touring the premises of an Iron Horse golf club.

"They've got them all over the country," says his wife, "and you have to own property on it to play the course." My next question feels stupid, but then, I figure, so is their need to play golf on an exclusive course up a mountainside.

"Couldn't you just play on the public course downtown? I mean, if you're only going to be here a couple months a year ..." And that's where my charitable view of this couple hits a pothole. Because there I am, wanting to move back to a home I love fiercely, yet facing the incomprehensible prospect of not being able to afford Montana. And there they are, willing to drop over half a million dollars to buy an empty quarter-acre lot so they can golf a particular eighteen holes once a year. How can my meager income compete with that? How can anyone's?

I am reminded of this couple when having lunch with one of my former high school teachers the next day. "I don't understand these people," his wife says. "There's this woman I know having trouble selling her 4300-square-foot house. She's got a driveway almost a mile long. Who in their right mind would want to plow that in winter?" The acquaintance, like many snowbirds, only lives in Whitefish in the summer. "What did she come here for in the first place?"

What *do* people come for? Some Montana mystique? The last best place? The lure of Western individualism? You might as well ask why people go anywhere at all.

The question is, what do I come for? What is this place I am hoping to return to, after years of living abroad and then on the East Coast with my English husband and our kids? How is my dream of Montana any different from theirs? The frontier is gone. The wilderness is sometimes preserved, sometimes not. The town is like towns all over the world—people pushing and pulling and rubbing along together, trying to build good lives for themselves and their children. Do I deserve the Big Sky more because they love it less? What do I think I'll find here, if I move back? What sort of magic could keep Montana secure from the rapacious spread of humanity?

*   *   *

"I need to get out of here," I say to Ian after three days. We've hiked up Big Mountain once, stuffing ourselves with this year's bumper wild huckleberry crop along the way. The rest of the time we drove around the countryside, as all the other tourists do, "looking at real estate," and I can't take anymore. The sight of log McMansion developments carving their way up once-empty mountainsides and gargantuan, hotel-sized homes on what were once the sites of human-sized farmhouses left me reeling. A speck of land on the lake, a place once perfect for communal high school bonfires, costs over a million dollars. I try to imagine my kids growing up here, whether they would have the slightest chance of absorbing the wilderness in their blood, something that I took for granted until coming back, and I feel as if I've been shot in the gut.

We drive out toward East Glacier, where my mother and I used to escape Whitefish's abnormally gray winters. The road winds along the bottom of Glacier National Park's big-shouldered mountains and shoots out onto the prairie like it's been loaded with gunpowder.

Here, on the Blackfeet reservation, little has changed. For how long, I wonder? The clouds brushstroke across the sky and the prairie warps into the mangled toes of the Rocky Mountains. Behind us, unfarmed hills hold yellowbell, pasqueflower, bitterroot: indigenous prairie flowers that were rare even before the specters of housing developments and oil drilling encroached on their remaining landscape. Just to the north is the Two Medicine formation, where I first fell in love with geology and dinosaurs, history learned from stone rather than books. To the east rolls the land where generations of my grandfathers scraped out boundaries of their wheat ranches.

It brings no relief to acknowledge that my great-great-grandparents inflicted a similar kind of harm on the Native American tribes and their landscape that I wail about in Whitefish: carving up grasslands and enclosing the prairie to plow it under for wheat and cattle. I might feel some tenuous connection to the people whose teepee rings still mark my second cousin's cattle fields, but I wouldn't know this landscape, wouldn't love it, if those whose home it was for centuries hadn't been pushed out to make room for people like my ancestors. In the end, the losers always seem to be those who love the land and their relationship with it the most, those who have little desire for more.

We drive along the craze-lined hills where few tourists penetrate and the wind talks only to cattle and horses and trees. We pass a sign for neglected road repairs. "Rough Break," it says in orange. No kidding.

*   *   *

In a life driven by a craving for culture shock, I never thought that the most difficult integration would be back into my own hometown. Years of living abroad, plus several more feeling like an alien on the U.S.'s East Coast, and now I don't know if I have the courage to return. I love Montana more than I ever have another person, and its alteration has hit me harder than the betrayal of any person could. It seems easier, now, to escape overseas, to learn a new language and culture anywhere else, than it does to come back and face the reality of fighting for a home whose spirit is dying.

Seeing the effects of wealthy influxes on my community, where prices are driving young people out, I am torn between a desire to move back right now, immediately, to throw myself into the yanking between hyper-development and preservation; and running away, somewhere overseas where I can just be an observer and chronicler in the trials of some other community. It's easier to be the invader than the mourner, to take on the role of the couple from Texas somewhere else, with less money, perhaps, but not with any more right to belong. It's easier to move to a place that can't hurt me.

But to renounce Montana entirely is unthinkable—I wish it could remain protected, so that I can wander, knowing home will always be there. For those of the pioneer spirit, there is nowhere left to run.

*   *   *

The day before we leave, Ian and I get up early, intent on one last hike and handfuls of huckleberries.

Partway up Big Mountain's hairpin turns (which are being widened and softened) is a lookout maintained by the forest service. Its loop road is almost unnoticeable and leads only to one picnic table set near a rock ledge. I used to come to this place in high school, early in the morning, latte in hand, to watch the sun lighten the valley and sip coffee in the near-silence of pine whispers.

The lookout is still there. But I stop, stunned, at the evidence of a new development being cut in right above it. The little loop is ripped up, the road mashed out for access to what will be more multi-million dollar homes, more evidence that even Big Sky country's open views are only for the wealthy.

I turn my back to it, gulping back sobs, craving this one small piece of my life to be left alone. My heart scrabbles to voice a cry of injustice: *Shouldn't this beauty belong to everyone?* We sit on the picnic table and Ian puts his arm around me. Lodgepole pines stand sentry over a plunging view that I wish desperately had no monetary value. Do I fight or run?

I think of other places I've lived in and fallen for, of Scotland's Outer Hebridean islands, of Moscow and Vienna, and the Australian Outback. Maybe I've carried my Montana dream to all of them, infused them with a love of my home that runs so deep it's almost like DNA. I'm scared to return, scared of the changes, scared of the pain. But home, for me, doesn't actually exist anywhere else.

On that cool August morning, the refrain of a song my mother once wrote comes back to me. In all the wide world, none of those other places have the pull of her simple words: "I'd rather give up heaven than Montana."

Eye of the Beholder

By Kim Kankiewicz

I wait in a lobby with purple carpet and rounded walls and a magazine rack stuffed with picture books. A fifty-gallon aquarium nests in a cubby four feet above the ground. Orange and green nursery school furniture occupies the central space, surrounded by clusters of adult-sized chairs. I am thirty-five years old and the only patient here without a parent.

My life story could be set in eye doctors' offices. I've been pinned by technicians to a reclining chair in Phoenix as my first ophthalmologist dropped atropine into my pupils. I've written fawning essays about an eye doctor in South Dakota who nicknamed me Trouper. I've leaned into tonometry machines in Iowa and Kansas, with medical students lined up to scrutinize me. I've mourned for an eye doctor in Minnesota who died of cancer. I've formed an uneasy friendship with the wife of an eye doctor in Nebraska who had an affair with his nurse. I learned I was pregnant from an ophthalmologist in Boulder reviewing pre-operative blood work.

In all those encounters, I've never been the right age for my eye clinic. As a child with glaucoma, I grew accustomed to being an anachronism. Among the crepe skin and hunched backs, I was pink cheeks and muscled legs. It was one of the ways my visual impairment made me uncomfortably visible.

I laugh when, two decades after my diagnosis, I find myself the lone adult patient in a room full of children sporting eye patches and doll-sized spectacles. The mother next to me, a nervous twenty-something, glances my way, and I pretend to be amused by the book I'm holding. I hadn't considered what should have been obvious when I scheduled this appointment: a specialist in strabismus, colloquially known as "lazy eye," is primarily a pediatric ophthalmologist.

This is confirmed when the doctor enters the exam room twenty minutes later. He is wearing a Mickey Mouse tie. He skims the pages in my fat file and wheels his chair over. We sit knee to knee as he shines a penlight into my blind eye, then studies it through a scope.

"Working around your other surgeries, I can get you to eighty percent alignment," he says.

"Would this be covered by insurance?" I can see nothing from my right eye, which is why it's wandered further off kilter every year since the surgery in my teens that marred my appearance without saving my sight.

"It's medically justifiable," the doctor says. There's some practical benefit: face-to-face communication would be less distracting for my conversation partners. And my blind eye takes in just enough light to claim a functional benefit.

Realistically, though, strabismus surgery won't improve my vision and isn't necessary. I knew this when I made the appointment. What I am contemplating is, for all intents and purposes, cosmetic surgery.

*　　*　　*

I once vowed, horrified when a classmate had breast implants before she was old enough to vote, that I would never opt for surgery that wasn't medically necessary. My smug self-assurance came from an unusually informed perspective. By my twenties, I'd lost count of the eye surgeries I'd endured. Enough to have preferences regarding anesthesia. (Fentanyl is nice.) I knew that surgery is always nightmarish, recovery always excruciating.

The collective experience of surgery made me feel like a cadaver, indifferently carved open and sewn back together. When the doctor in Boulder joked that mine was his first pregnancy announcement after screening for six thousand cataract operations, I wasn't impressed. I was just glad to be distinguishable from the other 5,999 patients.

Only on the operating table did I want my handicap to stand out. Everywhere else, I wanted to appear intact. I tried to achieve this by excelling in school, performing onstage, and ultimately starving and exercising my body until it collapsed and I left college for bulimia treatment. Eating disorders are complicated, their genesis complex, but I know mine originated between an exam chair where I squinted against the light and a school hallway where I wore sunglasses indoors, between a hospital bed where I wanted to be conspicuous and a waiting room where I did not.

Healing from an eating disorder is simultaneously complicated and simple. Recovery is a lifetime process, but it often comes down to treating oneself with both gentleness and brutal honesty. I've acknowledged my self-absorption, my complicity with a system that values women's adherence to narrow standards of beauty above all else. Most of the time, I resist preoccupation with my appearance by throwing balled-up socks at the television when a woman is blatantly objectified and asking myself who would possibly benefit if I were more attractive.

Who will benefit if my wonky right eye is aligned with the left one? I don't believe anyone has ever been too distracted by my lopsided gaze to maintain a coherent conversation with me. I suspect some acquaintances have not even noticed what feels to me like a huge deformity. Despite the growth I think I've experienced, I have to consider that in the end this surgery is nothing more than vanity.

* * *

The operation takes place at a children's hospital. The intake nurse, who rarely needs to differentiate between patient and child, talks to me in a high-pitched voice. Even when she catches herself, she seems unable to adjust her register. To add to her discomfiture, I am accompanied by my mother because my husband was called away on out-of-state business. My mother has experienced nearly as many eye surgeries as I have and is worried primarily about finding her way back to my house if I'm not lucid enough to navigate. She comforts me, unexpectedly, in a way my husband could not.

"It's a simple repair," she says. "Nothing to feel conflicted about."

Mothers don't cause eating disorders, but if you made a list of the ways they might contribute to them, very few of those factors would apply to my mom. She has an incomprehensibly easy relationship with food. She makes healthy choices as a way of life. I don't recall her uttering a single deprecating remark about her body or mine. The closest she came to criticizing my appearance was asking semi-regularly, "Is that what you're wearing today?" as if I'd donned a costume to amuse her before dressing in my actual clothes. (Retrospective photographic evidence explains her bewilderment.)

I didn't understand my own feelings about my eye disease, and I hid them from my mother. She hid from me the likelihood that I'd be blind before adolescence, the plan to relocate to a city with a blind school, the fears that she was inadequate to help me survive. What I saw was my parents' unwavering presence. Intuiting that my vision was at risk, I was unworried. My parents would take care of me. Little did I know my mother felt as insufficient as I did.

The surgery is not as simple as my mother predicts. Through the haze of anesthesia, the operating team's conversation sounds graver than usual. The operation, I later learn, lasts an hour longer than scheduled. When I awake, my surgeon explains that he discovered additional real estate left from previous operations. He'd altered his game plan to avoid damaging a shunt. In practical terms, this means more pain and less certainty of success.

It will be days before my eye turns from blood-red to white, weeks before I can peruse the lasting impact of surgery. Will it noticeably change my appearance? Will it change anything else?

"I'm glad you could be here," I tell my mom, when she has driven us home without a wrong turn.

"Me too," she says.

*   *   *

My children are solicitous when they return from a friend's house after my operation. This is their first brush with eye surgery, and their concern charms me. I explain the procedure as my mom defined it for me, as a repair. They don't know the surgery is an attempt to improve my appearance; I won't let on that I wish to be beautiful. It's an intermittent desire, one that no longer defines me, yet I've gone under the knife to satisfy it.

I want to spare my little girl from measuring her value in a mirror, but Signe is learning, inevitably, that beauty matters. She has confided that she hopes she is pretty enough to have friends in kindergarten. I stumbled through what I hoped was an appropriate response, enumerating the qualities that make her a good friend. She looked unconvinced.

When Signe stared at my face a few months before surgery, I thought of an essay by Alice Walker. Walker dreaded the day her daughter would notice her mother's disfigured eye, just as my daughter was noticing mine. The pivotal moment in Walker's essay is when her daughter remarks, "Mommy, there's a world in your eye." I shouldn't set much store by this atypically affectionate account of Walker's relationship with her now estranged daughter. Even so, I was crushed when my little girl said, "Your eye looks scary."

She recognized my hurt before I masked it and apologized for days afterward. I reassured her she'd done nothing wrong, talked about how differences make us beautiful, told her my blind eye reminded me to be grateful for the eye that can see. But she had observed that deep down, I too hope I'm pretty enough to belong.

You won't find *integral* as a synonym for *beautiful* in any thesaurus. In my vocabulary, they share meaning. *Integral* means both whole and essential to the whole. If you are integral, you are complete, and the world would not be complete without you. What I have learned over years of reflection is that when I long to be beautiful, I long to be integral.

*   *   *

Three weeks after surgery, my irises are horizontally aligned so closely you might think they were allies. The overall effect, however, is unremarkable. My right iris remains a paler shade of green than the left. My right pupil is still the black-marker dot of a child's drawing, never dilating because it never beholds light. My right eyelids, stretched and sliced over decades of treatment, still gape like snarled lips.

As a child, I heard a doctor say my disease could "burn out" by adolescence. I imagined a celebration, like a sweet sixteen party with balloons and cake, attended by my friends, my doctors, the aunts and uncles who inquired about my eyes during holiday dinners, the teachers who had visited me at the hospital. Now, as an adult who should have outgrown such naive fantasies, I had let myself believe again that a single moment in my ocular history could unbreak what came before.

Most days I am reconciled with the badge of my brokenness. Most days understanding my desire for beauty as a desire for wholeness is enough to make peace with it. Most days I believe I am integral to—and through—my mother and daughter and every woman who wants to be integral, too. But some days I close my eyes, unseeing and unseen, and dream of revision.

The Love of My Life, the Thief of My Sleep

By Sarah Werthan Buttenwieser

When he first started to stay over at our house, my then future-stepfather brought my mother a curious gift. It was a rather large brass horn, used by hunters, he said. The brass curled around itself; the flare of the horn was handsome. But it was odd, this object. We all stared at the horn and then at him when he presented it to her. The gift wasn't romantic, nor did it have to do with dreams of hunting trips. It was supposed to be practical. "If I snore too loudly," he explained, "just blow the horn."

My mother practically giggled at the gift. She certainly blushed. She mumbled something along the lines of his snoring being "not that bad." She was happy, that much was clear, and I was relieved and pleased for her.

By rights, though, he should have brought me a kazoo—or a fog-horn. His snores traveled through the ceiling of what had been her room and quickly became theirs right through my bedroom floor. He was, indeed, a loud snorer—the loudest, in fact, I've ever known. The sound resembled a cross between a drone and a series of honks. You could picture some cartoon character with a big bill or an outsized schnozz.

Their romance began near the end of my high school career and my leaving for college. The snoring served as a tiny sign to get out, a harbinger. Things were changing in the household. That was fine—I was ready to leave. Most of the time, I found the incredibly thunderous sounds from below more amusing than annoying. It was loud, but it was at a safe remove.

*　　*　　*

Years later, I met the love of my life. It turns out that Hosea, too, snores. His snoring is a honking, snuffly, schnozzy, start-and-stop affair. Sometimes, it reminds me of a monologue, comedic to the listener, dramatic to the performer. Except the performer sleeps through it and the listener finds herself in a tragedy, the one of being awake to hear it in the middle of the night. I can't say whether he snored less early in our relationship or whether I was so entirely smitten for the first decade and a half that I just didn't care. I care now.

My boyfriend-turned-husband displayed an uncanny ability to sleep through anything. Hosea snored and he slept, the one never disturbing the other. At the beginning of our relationship, in fact, I was in the midst of a kitchen renovation that required some work on the roof just beneath my bedroom. Think hammers that pounded loud enough to seem as if the work were going on inside your bedroom. He slept right through the ruckus morning after morning, long after the sun rose high in the sky. My usual wakeup time was more in the dawn hours and so I'd go about my day, incredulous that neither heavy construction nor full sun woke him. He often worked into the wee hours; he wasn't a slacker. Our opposite tendencies had advantages from the perspective of an early riser: Hosea didn't bother me when I did my best work, because he was fast asleep during my most cherished work hours.

When we became parents, his natural night owlish tendencies cut both. Chicken or egg, the first baby was a night owl, too. They hung out—and the baby slept in, once he was old enough not to wake up all day and night long. We had to wake him for preschool. On the positive side, the middle-of-the-night stuff could fall to my dear husband before he'd actually want to go to sleep. On the negative side, every early morning waking—with each child, the hours got more "kid normal"—fell to me and my precious early mornings evaporated. Back on the up side, Hosea can drive teenagers at night and recently chaperoned a cast party at our house that began at one a.m. and ended at four. I slept through the entire shebang. Also on the up side: I tend to go to bed before he does. Often, he's in bed, reading, and turns the light off for the two minutes it takes for me to drift off. That's sweet—quiet and sweet.

I've come to imagine snoring is much like the ripeness of high school and college-age males. Back when our bodies first discovered one another's, the funky ripeness became part of the appeal. A strong scent was a strong sensation. Their funk was, when we were together, mine in a way.

At some moment over the last few years, when the very dear and lovely and loud husband's snoring woke me, I ceased to be charmed—or forgiving. I went from unflustered to fully furious with flip-of-a-switch speed. I'd poke him. "You're so loud!" I'd call out, not quite yelling but certainly not whispering. Whispers had no impact at all. I needed to put more muscle into my voice than was readily available in the middle of the night, which is part of why I got so enraged. Ginger prods did not rouse him either. I had to poke or shake. This required *effort*. The act of attempting to get him to roll over or shut up woke me up *more*, after I'd already been awoken by his sonorous snores. This was a recipe for a trip to nowhere good and quickly.

Every next snore that he snored once I was awake and trying to get him to stop snoring just pissed me off even more. This assault on my sleep, after years of babies and toddlers and anxiety over the babies and toddlers, was kind of a final straw. I didn't want to be bothered by my husband. All those parenting hours that had chipped away at our alone time and our romance time were compounded in the middle of the night by his being the one to steal my rest from me. It was the opposite of romantic. It was burdensome and enraging.

Still, divorce did not enter my mind.

I began to fantasize about separate rooms. Sometimes, when it gets bad, Hosea shifts to a kid's bed or the couch in the room off our bedroom. Sometimes, if a kid has already moved into our bed, he'll simply take the kid's bed. Mostly, though, he prefers our bed and his position beside me. Lucky me. I mean that, you know, except for the sleeplessness. "Would separate rooms help?" he asked one morning after I hadn't slept much at all. "If that's what it takes, let's do it. It's not like we're doing anything in our bed at night surrounded by all these children other than sleeping.

"Sleeping," he added, "if we're lucky."

It was practically the most romantic offer ever made under the circumstances. I felt cared for and understood. Our romance remains alive, despite all those children. Our love is strong. Partners in exhaustion (and often in anxiety, too), we both covet ever-elusive sleep. Regardless of whether I'd like my own bedroom—and I know I'm not the only woman to want one—the truth is we don't have an extra bedroom.

*   *   *

After years of practice, Hosea responds pretty well to being jostled. I don't have to shake so hard or poke so pokily or yell so loud. "I'm sorry," he mumbles whenever I have to do so. He is, I know he is, as he slumbers on and I lie awake for a while. Unromantic as snoring is, insomnia is pretty much of a mood dampener as well. Some nights I lie awake, perplexed that I'm awake and that what bothers me are such silly things as snoring—or teenagers' socks strewn across the floor or loads of other things I never thought I'd be bothered by, for that matter. I don't know what I thought would preoccupy me. It just wasn't stuff like this.

Rather than simply have me furious at him every single night, we began to seek solutions. Hosea wears anti-snoring nose strips when he sleeps. They resemble Band-Aids. Some nights, they really help; other nights, they seem decorative, like the Dora the Explorer Band-

Aids my daughter insists on wearing. After years of my badgering, Hosea finally visited an allergist. The allergist identified allergies and prescribed new medication. The snoring has decreased in frequency and audibility.

The white noise machine I bought to help drown him out helps some, too, although not once I'm in awake and especially not once I'm kicked into worried mode. My mother's white noise machine is the public radio station, which drones on all night long—and serves the secondary purpose of distraction if she wakes up anxious. Also, my son notes her hearing isn't quite what it used to be. We got into her car recently—the radio blasting—and I'd have to agree with him. I guess I'm still hopeful that, like my mother has somehow done, I will eventually reach a state of accepting accommodation in regards to my husband's snoring. She continues to insist it's "not that bad." Hosea hasn't gotten me a horn, and I haven't begun to lose my hearing, not even selectively.

———

In Praise of Synthetic Vaginas

by Catherine Newman

Because a blow-up doll will surely take up too much room in the bed, what I really want is a syngina. You'll want one too, trust me. Go ahead and Google it. You're going to be like, "Wait! I'm not a tampon manufacturer needing to test absorbency!" That's okay. I'm not either. My interest in a synthetic vagina is purely personal. I plan to deploy it as an occasional stand-in for my real vagina, the same way a college may hire an adjunct to replace a professor on sabbatical—with the sabbatical being taken, in this case, by my own weary crotch.

Heterosexuality is a bizarre and perverted phenomenon. Whose idea was it to combine reproduction with sex? Because it was a bad one. At forty-four, after more extreme reproductive experiences than you could count on my nipple hairs, sex feels about as festive to me as a Ferris wheel erected in a cemetery. It's thrilling, sure, and the views are great, but it's also just plain weird, and sometimes kind of sad and scary.

In the twenty-five years that Michael and I have been together, I have peed on one gazillion pregnancy tests, give or take. I have thrilled to positive and negative results both, to plus signs and minus signs, double lines and single lines and subtle ombre shiftings of color, as well as the subtle absence of this shifting of color, from white to blue, or white to pink, or white to some other shade of white, and "Honey, are these two colors the same color or not?" ("Um. You mean the white and, uh, the white?") I have also wept over positive and negative results both. I have thrilled to a positive test, my heart briefly soaring, mere moments before sighing and picking up the phone to call Planned Parenthood. I have wept over a negative pregnancy test, cried for the baby I didn't want but now wouldn't get to have, mere moments after clasping my hands in prayer that it would be negative.

Wanted pregnancies have devolved into bloody phlegm, me on my hands and knees on the bathroom tiles, keening, or me propped up in bed, munching on a donut with sticky equanimity. Unexpected pregnancies have progressed into toast-induced vomiting and colossally pendulous hemorrhoids, and then into babies who braced themselves stubbornly against my pelvis and had to be forcibly excavated with scalpels and sections, my belly traversed by a transcontinental railroad of staples and stitches. An unwanted pregnancy was terminated with suction and ad hoc Slavic-inflected counseling ("You khev heared of diaphragm?"), with a stupor of grief and relief and Valium, watching *The Bird Cage* with Michael and snorting laughter out of my nose at all the funny parts. "You would normally have hated this movie," he said, and I said, "I know," and shrugged pleasantly from beneath the drugs. Grief morphed briefly into regret, morphed back, later, to relief. (That anybody would use the fact of grief or regret as an argument against reproductive rights always strikes me as short-sighted. Should every potentially regrettable choice be illegal? Marriage, paint colors, teetery t-strap sandals? Having sex or a baby? Ordering a second basket of fries or a third mojito?)

I have squinted at an ultrasound with my mystified gynecologist until she clapped and said "There!" and pointed to the IUD listing over at the edge of my withered whoopee cushion of a uterus. "Probably not a great fit for you," she said, adding, superfluously, "birth-control-wise."

I have had allergic reactions in the vagina, to latex, lambskin, and spermicide. I have had literally *dozens* of yeast infections and figuratively *millions* of UTIs. When I explained to my ten-year-old daughter that women get more bladder infections than men, she said, wisely, "Well sure. With women, it's like you're walking right into the house. Men have a kind of a mudroom."

My body is a wonderland. If, by "wonderland," you mean mismatched breasts like a hedgehog family's deflating air mattresses. If you mean brown, rubbery nipples that appear to have been pilfered from a 1970s-era baby bottle before getting glued on. It's not just regular aging—like the fact that my neck looks like somebody's ill-cared-for scrotum. It's not the constellations of moles and acne and wrinkles, like a crazed galaxy spanning multiple eons. It's that my body is like a beautiful and terrible reproductive neighborhood. Sexuality is in the mix, sure, but it's a flowering window box on a condemned building, with the wrecking ball swinging noisily in the background.

I weep and rage. I'm sad sometimes, or overcome with joy. I fill up, spill over with nostalgia: These silver C-section scars! These golden children! The blinding lights of my life, who bring me to my knees with love, a thousand times a second. I shudder and burst into tears and cry until I laugh.

And Michael? Michael just comes and comes. He has experienced this same twenty-five years as a more or less happy collection of orgasms, as if he's the simple hydraulic version of a senselessly complicated machine. He has also seduced and delighted, to be sure. Baffled and alarmed, he has held me while I wept. He has fathered two beautiful children in a beautiful way. But for him, sex is still about, of all things, *pleasure*. It is not a holy act of grief-stricken joy. It is not exhibit A in a report about PTSD, or a tearful, garter-belted clown in a postmodern circus. He does not cling to my neck, weeping, "This is how we made our *babies*." His cheerful seed sprays hither and yon. And I hate to begrudge him.

Thus the syngina. I'll put my novel down, even, and turn towards him willingly, my fake vagina at the ready. I won't worry, for the thirtieth year in a row, about getting pregnant. I won't experience full-body flashbacks. I'll just smile and encourage and my vagina will wink at me, like a retiring police horse, before its blameless and well-earned rest.

———
———

Land of Shannon

By Suzanne Van Atten

Bone tired and drunk on whiskey, I was wedged in the corner of a booth at Gus O'Connor's Pub in the small seaside town of Doolin, Ireland. I watched my three girlfriends chat up an international coterie of men who had flocked to our table, drawn to the trio of boozed-up beauties. A decade older than my friends and more plain, I was excluded from the sexual energy that emanated from their flirtatious repartee, and I turned my attention to the musicians who filled the air with the sometimes jaunty, sometimes mournful sounds of their guitars, fiddles, and accordion. I recently had grown accustomed to my place in the periphery of my friends' mating dance.

For years I had been a suburban divorced mom, occupied by working as an arts editor for the local newspaper and raising two sons mostly on my own. But that all changed when my youngest son left home for college. I decided my life needed a shakeup, so I broke up with my boyfriend of twelve years and moved into the city. Although a mere ten miles separated my former home (a '60s ranch house in a working-class neighborhood) from my new abode (a shabby Victorian duplex in the shadow of glass-and-steel high-rises), they were worlds apart.

The moving van had barely pulled away from the curb when I found myself thrust into a lifestyle more like that of a college freshman than a divorced mom in her late-forties. A simple invitation to a colleague's house party was my entrée into a lively social circle of mostly thirty-something journalists and publicists who threw raucous parties, went to clubs to hear bands, and closed down bars three and four nights a week. Seemingly overnight, my phone was ringing with invitations to meet my new friends for drinks, dinner, and more. I soon developed an impressive tolerance for alcohol consumption and a constant quest for the perfect concealer to hide the permanent dark circles beneath my eyes.

One night after work, I met my friend Shelly for a beer at our favorite neighborhood bar. A flirtatious redhead with a penchant for floral print sundresses and red lipstick, Shelly is the most extroverted of my friends and the ringleader of our social activities. Her perpetually cranky boyfriend had recently moved out of the duplex they'd shared for six years and taken up with an art school student nineteen years his junior. Since her breakup, we occasionally lamented our single status. We missed having someone to share our beds, to kill our bugs, to carry out our trash; lately what we missed most was our traveling companions. That's when we came upon the idea of taking a trip together. I had been dreaming of Ireland, and that suited Shelly, so we decided to book a trip in March.

We invited two friends to join us: Amy, the marketing director for the newspaper where I worked, a short, curvy blonde with an infectious giggle and dimples to match, and Scottie, an advertising executive at a global marketing firm, a tall, willowy, strawberry blonde. Amy recently had broken up with her boyfriend, a cute bald-headed boy and utilities trader who had become so obsessed with online gambling he no longer left his apartment. Scottie had been on her own for years, having yet to recover from the day she returned to her elegant, antiques-and-art-filled home to find her trust fund-baby boyfriend of seven years in bed with another woman.

Over a round of drinks one night, we raised our glasses to toast the fact that we were independent women with disposable income who didn't need men by our sides to see the world.

* * *

Our journey began in Dublin, where we spent our days touring the usual sights—museums, churches and shops—and our nights were spent in the pubs where I often found myself shuttled to the side as men elbowed their way in to chat up the girls. Sometimes I would return to the table from a visit to the restroom to find my chair taken by another potential suitor. There was a time when I would have been in that game, I thought, but it appeared that time had passed.

But then, I'd look at these men—overgrown boys really—with their drunken swagger and imbecilic conversations laced with crude double entendres, and I'd wonder why my friends bothered. Especially knowing the night would end on a sour note when the pub closed and the men realized my friends were just having a bit of fun and were going home alone.

After a couple of days in Dublin, we planned to spend the rest of our stay in Galway, but first was the leg of our trip I had anticipated most. I was leading the charge on a 250-mile roundtrip driving tour south of Galway through the picturesque Dingle Peninsula and back north again to spend the night in Doolin, a tiny seaside town famous for its pubs and the local musicians who gather there to play traditional Irish music.

The day of our journey, we woke up early and went to the hotel dining room for breakfast where I scanned the morning paper over a plate of bacon and eggs. "Listen to this," I said, as I relayed the lead story. A man convicted of raping a divorced mother of three had been set free on probation, and his victim, Mary Shannon, had gone public to renounce the light sentence. Activists were rallying around her, and a protest march was planned in her hometown of Ennis. We studied the photograph of Mary Shannon, her long brown hair framing a face etched with anger.

"Unbelievable!" I said. "He was found guilty!"

"I guess you can get away with rape in Ireland," said Shelly.

We finished our breakfast and the girls sipped a round of mimosas in the hotel lobby while I negotiated the terms with the car rental agent, a blustery, red-faced man straight out of central casting whose brogue was so thick, I barely understood a word he said. After his interminable lecture on the car's operating systems, we took our positions—me behind the wheel, Shelly in the passenger seat with a map on her lap, and Amy and Scottie in the back seat. Off we set.

"Stay left, stay left!" "Watch the curb!" were Shelly's constant refrains the first hour or so of our drive. Any other time I would have been annoyed, but mastering the art of driving on the left was no easy task and I welcomed her warnings. It couldn't have been a more beautiful, sunny day, despite the March chill, and we admired the lovely green countryside, the low-slung stone walls and the charming little towns we passed as we headed south. But traversing the narrow, winding roads proved more time consuming than we had imagined, and three hours into our journey we found ourselves in a quandary. Our progress had been slow and time was passing; we began to wonder if we could cover all the ground we had hoped to in one day.

We stopped in the village of Camp, the northern gateway to Dingle Peninsula, and studied the map. It indicated a coastal road that looped around the land mass and a cut-through that dissected it called Conor Pass, at the end of which was the village of Dingle. If we drove the circumference of the peninsula, could we get to Doolin in time to make it to the pubs?

"Well, we've made it to Dingle Peninsula. We could just turn around and go back now," said Shelly.

"The point was not to just come here," I protested. "I want to actually see it. Maybe we could just drive along the northern route a bit, then turn around and head back."

As precious minutes ticked by, Shelly and I debated our options and studied the map while Amy and Scottie sat quietly in the back seat. The more laid-back half of our quartet had been content so far to let the two alpha-chicks in the front seat call the shots. But we had reached an impasse.

"We've come this far. I think we should at least drive through Conor Pass," Scottie said.

So we all agreed and proceeded along the northern route of Dingle Peninsula, speeding as fast as the narrow road would allow and climbing dramatically in altitude. Before long we noticed there was not another car in sight, not a house, not a road marker, not a sign of civilization anywhere.

"Look behind us!" Amy shouted, and we all looked back at the sunny, grassy, low-lying plains rimmed by the sea now far below us. It was a splendid sight, but it did not prepare us for what was to come. No sooner did we fix our eyes back on the road ahead that we rounded a sharp curve that revealed a vastly different vista.

Like some sort of eerie, lunar landscape, Conor Pass lay before us: a rollercoaster of massive stone mountains as far as the eyes could see. One after another, they rolled toward the horizon, all gray and rounded and rocky. We wound our way through the mountains, around enormous boulders that looked poised to roll over on us at any moment. Along the way were wide spots in the road where we pulled over to get out of the car and run up and down natural stepping-stones that led toward barren mountaintops. We rubbed our fingertips over thick carpets of fuzzy mosses and teal-colored lichen that grew in nooks and crevices around the rocks. We wet our hands in natural spigots of rushing cold water that splashed out of holes in the mountain, creating small pools and streams.

The wind grew fierce atop Conor Pass, so we pulled out every coat, scarf and cap we could find in the trunk to bundle up, and we ran around in circles like little kids to warm up, snapping pictures in every direction. The bitter cold and bizarre beauty made me feel drunk and giddy, and I was struck by the sensation that we were alone in the universe, plunked down in a place completely otherworldly and wholly our own.

Back in the car, we descended down the road, and the landscape gave way once again to lush green pastures and views of the southern coastline on the horizon. We stopped in the town of Dingle, where we shared a round of pints at Dick Mack's Pub before starting along the peninsula's southern route. That was when hunger pangs grabbed hold, reminding us that our breakfast had been so many hours ago.

As we approached the end of Dingle Peninsula, we entered the town of Annascaul and spotted The South Pole Inn. It was a ramshackle, two-story pub with fires burning in the hearth and walls lined with vintage photographs and newspaper clippings chronicling the South Pole expeditions of local explorer Tom Crean. Several photographs depicted the big strapping adventurer dressed in parka and pelts standing on a stark, vast landscape as seemingly unworldly as that which we had just left behind on Conor Pass.

Mindful of the time, we ordered our food to go—four toasted ham and cheese sandwiches and a single pile of fried chips. As we sped down the road, we perched the box of potatoes on the console between the front seats and devoured the warm, mushy triangles of meat and cheese.

The sun was no longer visible in the sky but daylight clung on, and I sped as fast as I could, hoping the light would last until we made the River Shannon, where we had to catch a car ferry.

"Um," Amy uttered from the backseat. I glanced in the rearview mirror and saw her nose buried in the ferry schedule. "Yeah," she said solemnly. "The last ferry is at 7:30 p.m."

"What?" I cried. "It can't be! The schedule says there's one at 8:30 and 9:30, too!" But I was wrong. I had misread the timetable, mistaking the summer schedule for the shorter off-season one. I looked at the dashboard clock while my toasted ham and cheese sandwich tumbled uncomfortably in my stomach.

"It's 6:30 now." I said. "There's no way we'll make it."

I was answered by silence.

"We can make it!" Shelly finally said with forced cheer. She studied the map for a few minutes. "Yeah, we can do it."

If we missed the ferry, it would add ninety minutes to our drive over unfamiliar roads in the dark and would mean missing out on the pubs in Doolin, which closed promptly at midnight. We had no choice but to fly as fast as we could. I tightened my grip on the steering wheel and said a silent prayer: "Please don't let us die trying."

Between towns we zoomed past slow-moving vehicles and straddled the middle of the road on straight-aways at a fast clip. Outside Tralee, we came upon a moving roadblock. Despite our haste, we delighted at the sight of it: a man and his two children herding a trio of black-and-white cows down the road to a fresh pasture.

The clock read 6:43.

Our progress was slowed as we passed through the tiny towns along the way—Tralee and Listowel and Tarbert. We navigated our way around the confusing roundabouts. In Listowel we exited on the wrong road, but realized our error and backtracked through the traffic circle and headed the right way.

It was 7:12.

The last glint of light left the sky as we passed though Tarbert and headed down the final stretch to the ferry docks — a long, narrow, winding road with hairpin turns along the way. Everyone was silent and tense with concentration as though we could propel ourselves there by the combined force of our will. The clock read an impossible 7:24. The road was thickly wooded and our high-beams cut a swath through the darkness as I took curve after curve. My arms and shoulders were as tense as steel rods as I gripped the wheel and negotiated the tight turns.

"Maybe they'll see our lights coming and wait," I offered hopefully.

As we came around the last curve, the woods gave way, and we spotted the brightly lit station where the ferry waited, idling quietly at the dock. I shouted with joy as I zoomed on board and eased on the brakes, slipping into our space in the orderly row of cars and trucks calmly waiting to cross to the other side.

It was 7:31.

I rolled down the glass as the ticket-taker briskly approached my window, and I started to fumble with my purse to find my pre-purchased ticket.

"May I take your pulse, please?" he said with a wink.

We piled out of the car to stretch our cramped limbs. While the girls ran off to the restroom, I braved the fierce wind to climb up the steps to the viewing deck and watched the lights of the ferry dock fade into the night as we motored toward the north shore. My heart was still racing from the harrowing drive and my nose and fingers were numb with cold, but I relished the few minutes alone. I could barely believe we had made it. It was just a ferry crossing, but it felt like something more—like a test or a challenge, and I had won. Age may be robbing me of whatever grace and beauty I might have once had, I thought as I stood in the middle of the dark river, but I had guts and drive to spare, damn it. And that counted for something; in fact, it counted for a lot. For the first time I had the freedom and capacity to live a life of my own design, and I was just now realizing what an immense gift that was.

The tension that had chased us to the River Shannon had lessened somewhat, but we were still fighting the clock. The pubs closed at midnight and it would take us at least two hours to get to Doolin. Luckily, the roadways were nearly empty, and I straddled the middle line to avoid the low-slung rock walls that lined the streets and threatened to stop us, literally, dead in our tracks.

Driving as fast as I could, we passed through the dairy lands of County Clare in dark silence. But when we entered the last town before our final trek along the isolated back roads to Doolin, our progress was stopped cold at the town's main crossroads. My intent was to turn right, but if I had, we would have been thrust headlong into an approaching procession of women and children slowly marching toward us carrying lit candles in their hands. Flanked by two women carrying a banner that read, "Stop domestic abuse," I could just make out the unmistakable figure of a tall thin woman with long brown hair leading the way.

"My God, it's Mary Shannon," I said.

Struck by the solemn dignity of the women's flame-lit faces as they silently approached, I was overcome by a sense of solidarity. I shared their outrage and admired them for claiming their right to be heard. And I identified with their desire for safety. I was suddenly aware that we were a group of women traveling alone in a foreign land, tempting danger as we sped through the night over unfamiliar roads and chatted up strangers over one too many pints. Our concerns were focused on making sure our money held out and cramming in everything we wanted to do before our time was up—not just in Ireland but in our lives back home, too.

We were city girls who lived in sketchy neighborhoods where panhandlers, car break-ins, and unwanted attention were daily occurrences. We patronized convenience stores buttressed with bulletproof glass to withdraw twenties from ATMs so we could go to dive bars where we stayed out too late. Afterward, we walked to our cars alone in the dark, returning to our burglar-barred homes, where we slept soundly in our beds, secure—however falsely—in the notion that we were safe.

"Quick, turn left," Shelly said. "We've got to get around them."

I followed her commands as she directed me around the women and back on our route north. Soon Mary Shannon and her band of supporters were far behind, along with the fears they embodied—of physical harm, vulnerability, financial instability, loneliness—the fears so many single women suppress every day without even thinking about it in order to get through the day.

Eventually we began to descend into the tiny coastal town of Doolin. It was not difficult to find the Sea View B&B; there were only three streets in town. When we spotted the little dormered house stuck in the side of a hill, I couldn't park the car and empty the trunk fast enough. Being the most eager to hit Gus O'Connor's Pub—happily visible just across the creek not 100 yards away—I was the first one to clamber up the steps of the house and drop the brass knocker on the wooden door.

A post I'd read on a blog back home about a traveler being turned away from the Sea View for arriving too late flickered in the back of mind.

Again I dropped the knocker.

I heard rustling inside and a stomp or two, then the door flung open to reveal a very angry proprietress, wearing a thin floral bathrobe cinched tight to her waist with one hand, her blonde wiry curls bunched wildly in tufts on her head.

"You might have called," she barked.

I apologized profusely as the others trundled in behind me, heavy with bags and fatigue.

"You'll be heading to the pubs I guess," she said.

We dropped our bags in our ruffled, rose-print bedrooms, ran combs through our hair and flew out the door, down the steep steps, over the stone bridge and into Gus O'Connor's Pub. Finally! The time had come to toast our adventure and hear some Irish tunes.

The tightly packed bar was teeming with people, young and old, who were not just looking for a good time but had clearly found it. A fire burned in a hearth in the corner of the anteroom, and on the walls were scores of photographs of musicians and instruments.

We stepped into the large, main room, lined on one side by a long bar on the left. On the right, the space was filled with small tables and chairs, every one occupied. In the center of the room seated on chairs and benches were five musicians playing guitars, fiddles, flutes, and an accordion. We lingered by the bar with our first round, soaking in the music, before grabbing a booth just as a large group left.

We weren't there long before we were joined by a revolving cast of young men, all travelers from various parts of the world. There was much talk about an upcoming rugby match they were eager to see the next day. We chatted and laughed, stepped outside to share cigarettes, and drank rounds of Guinness and whiskey. The muscles in my shoulders burned a bit as they slowly began to unfurl, releasing the tension that had gripped them all day. The whiskey was warm and soothing in my belly.

My mind soon wandered from the boys and their brash talk about where they were from and where they were going. I turned my attention to the music and grew fascinated by the deep red accordion as it wheezed and moaned its sad, lovely songs. A young woman smitten with its player had convinced him to let her fondle the instrument between songs. I had a powerful desire to wrap my hands around the mysterious contraption, to finger the small knobs and gently pump its lung as it wheezed. I wanted so badly to join them so I, too, could get a turn to touch the buttons and curious folds. Instead I just watched them from afar as they manipulated the instrument and felt my throat thicken with longing.

When the band was done for the night, I turned back toward my friends. Scottie was deep in quiet conversation with a beautiful, dark-eyed Italian, their heads so close together they nearly touched. Amy giggled as two animated Brits told her an elaborate story that required frantic hand gestures. Shelly, her eyes bright and her lips awash in a swipe of red, was snuggled up to a very tall Irish man with a goofy mustache. So I drained my glass, pulled on my coat and walked back to the Sea View alone in the dark.

The Return of the Dropout

By Sara Bir

In three hours, I have a chemistry exam I might fail. I say "might" because I could cram desperately in the three hours between this moment and the time of my probable failing, and I'd rather spend those three hours doing something useful. Cramming is a deceptive word for panicking.

This feeling of looming academic doom is familiar, and I'm skilled at managing it calmly. Somehow I passed chemistry when I took it in high school, over twenty years ago. ("Somehow" was actually Betsy, my saintly lab partner, who happened to be the daughter of a chemistry teacher.) I recall very little about our curriculum—octets and ions and moles—but I remember sitting close to the window, because through it I observed the antics of a brazen woodchuck that lived in the woods bordering the school grounds. I also remember looking at the graffiti on my desk, which read, "Paige and Erin are DIKES." They were not, as I knew firsthand, because Paige and Erin were two of my best friends. I also knew how to spell dykes properly, with a Y instead of an I, but it took me a few weeks of staring at the doubly incorrect slur on the desk before I realized I could simply erase it. If high school chemistry had tested me on groundhogs and stupid rumors and the ability to sketch various martyred saints in my notebook while listening to the Doors, I would have received an A.

And now, this exam nears. All these years later, I thought I had learned my lesson about chemistry class. Unlike the first time, I have applied myself as much as possible, because the topic is genuinely interesting to me—or at least the parts that have to do with cooking, because I am a chef. I'm teaching a charcuterie class next week, and deadlines loom: finish typing up the recipe packet, order duck legs and duck fat, drive all over town to purchase ingredients. Chemistry and charcuterie both require my full attention. My heart is with the pig.

Charcuterie is the art of preserving meat, most often through curing, smoking, or drying. Different chemical reactions make it all possible, sodium and nitrogen compounds mingling and swapping electrons in atomic versions of French kisses and extravagant, multi-player sexual positions. $NaCl$. $NaNO_2$. KNO_3.

Of course, I can't write balanced chemical equations for what happens when you rub kosher salt, brown sugar, and sodium nitrite on a slab of fresh pork belly and let it sit for a week or so (some juniper berries, peppercorns, sage, and bay leaves are helpful, too). I just know that it happens. You put the dry cure on, flip the belly over every day to make sure it cures evenly, and, five to eight days later, it's bacon. (You can omit the sodium nitrite, and the myoglobin in the meat won't turn that hammy pink color, but the end result will still be delicious.) Then you rinse off the dry cure, at which point you can smoke it or cook it off in the oven. It's not rocket science, but it *is* chemistry. What you wind up with is different from what you started out with.

* * *

Always chemistry awaits. Chemistry awaits because I don't have a Bachelor's Degree. I never wanted one, ever. I didn't even understand the difference between an Associate's Degree and a Bachelor's Degree when I went off to college, because I thought college was for browsing for used cassette tapes at record stores and drinking gallons of coffee at noisy cafes while reading a stack of the local alternative weekly newspapers. I dropped out of college before I failed, which is like quitting a job right before they can fire you. This didn't comfort my parents, whose money I had been wasting with great indifference. As it turned out, the money-wasting was merely an annoyance to them; their main concern, understandably, was my future.

My first paid writing job was for an alternative weekly newspaper, where I wrote music criticism. And so my parallel, independent course of study paid off somewhat, and for many years I was smug about it: *I don't have a traditional college degree and I never needed it, nah nah nah nha boo-boo!* College was for amateurs, people who like to sit and talk. Working? That's for pros. I'm a worker. I suck at sitting. That's why I went to cooking school.

Writers sit a lot, however. Despite my deep love for alternative weeklies, I left that job and undertook a string of high-energy, low-wage positions that managed to more or less pay the bills. Chocolate factory. Cookware store. Library. Introducing a daughter into this equation was financially irresponsible, but we did it anyway, on purpose.

Then I realized how flawed my logic was, and how pathetic and passive my budget-driven melancholy was. My husband, a likewise melancholic fellow with a meandering career background, was not going to bring home slabs of bacon, ever. I felt our lives slipping away from us as friends moved ahead into promised lands of financial security; we languished behind, tossing scraps at the incredibly persistent credit card balance we couldn't knock out, no matter how many extra hours I picked up at whatever job I was working at the time. In order for our family to make it, I needed to become a different person, one who could gracefully eat shit. A person who could bite the bullet and follow directions she didn't really want to follow.

* * *

We don't discuss charcuterie in chemistry. It's an online class, which I chose because my work schedule is unpredictable. There's a massive, poorly organized textbook, and we're supposed to read the textbook, log in to the web portal, and take half a dozen quizzes every week. That's it. When I emailed my instructor and asked her to recommend some resources outside of the book, she suggested I come to her lecture. "But I'm taking the class online," I said. "The lecture is supposed to come to me."

We do take our tests in person, and that's when I see our instructor, who is perhaps my age, with a petite build, an awkward manner, and a head of fabulously curly blonde hair. She seems to have a genuine concern for the academic performance of her students and a genuine difficulty connecting to them conversationally. I think she's as confident leading the class as I am taking it.

So there it is: I will probably fail the test, because instead of attending chemistry lectures after work, I'd rather rake leaves with my daughter and watch her jump in and out of the leaf piles with unmitigated three-year-old glee. I'd rather walk the dog before dinner with my husband, and we will push our daughter in the stroller with us even though she's way too old for the stroller and has to be coaxed into it with tiny handfuls of raisins or almonds, because if my husband and I don't move around and talk about our days in the neutral air of the outdoors, bad things will happen. I'd rather set a real table with cloth napkins and cook a real dinner, which we will sit down together to enjoy, because that's what we do in our family. I'd rather get my proper eight hours of sleep most nights, because if I don't, bad things happen.

Most of the kids in my chemistry lab could realistically be my kid. All these years later and I still can't make myself care enough to pass. Or maybe I care too much. Every week that infernal textbook throws more and more concepts at us, just when the one we were covering started to get really good. If it were up to me, I'd overhaul first-year chemistry and rename it Periodic Table Studies. I love the periodic table. It's like a beautiful map; with each examination, it reveals more intricacies, more patterns. There's a mysticism to it, a leap of faith, because I don't care how many experiments chemists have done over the past dozen centuries, we can't see and touch the atoms of those elements the way we can, say, a handful of cumin seeds or a stick of butter. Or a slab of pork belly.

I spent hours making flash cards for each element, because our instructor said we'd need to memorize most of the table. My inner child leapt for joy—craft time! I wrote the Latin or Greek roots of the names, or the interesting places they were discovered, plus short descriptions of what each element looked or smelled like, so it could be more tangible. Each element had its own story. I like narratives, and so far chemistry had not given me any good ones. On the day of our second exam, I was dismayed to find we were in fact not tested on our knowledge of the periodic table, but had to fill out a long list of electron configuration problems. And yes, those do have to do with the periodic table, but not in the way I like. By the time we hurtled to those, I was still swooning over radium and rubidium.

*   *   *

I went back to school with the ultimate goal of becoming a registered dietician. I have a culinary degree; I care about good nutrition; I love teaching cooking classes. I threw those things into a hat with my desired salary, spent a few weekends clicking away hopefully on the Occupational Outlook Handbook database, and—*poof!*—created my future, reasonably profitable career. The logic went like this: by the time I have my credentials, the job market for R.D.s will be extra-sweet because of the awful diets Americans have, my years of studying late into the night would pay off, and I'd be able take our family on nice vacations and finally fulfill my dream of pledging to multiple public radio stations.

I'll be nearing fifty by then. Is it worth it? Foremost I am a chef and a writer; I intentionally cook with bacon grease and chicken fat, I use salt liberally but strategically, and I'd rather discuss how to get a good sear on a pan of mushrooms than how to best preserve their nutrient content. That many R.D.s don't actually work with the public but create crummy, bland menus for giant institutions was something I chose to overlook.

Maybe failing chemistry is necessary. I'm stubborn, and I don't like to accept that I can only accomplish so much in a given time frame. Those cloth napkins are one reason we have so much laundry to fold. I have quite an array. Some I purchased for a song on clearance. Some I sewed myself in the days when I did a lot of freelance writing. I thought sewing napkins was procrastinating, but it turns out it's one of my preferred methods of prewriting. Ages have passed since I've made napkins, but I really enjoy using them. They make me feel especially civilized.

Using paper napkins would save me maybe a few hours of laundry chores every year, and I could use those hours to study chemistry. Instead, my pro-napkin actions have clearly voted against chemistry and all it stands for. Sometimes you can't just dip your toe in. You have to wade up to your ankles and hang out for a while before you realize that body of water is not where you are supposed to be.

This morning, I saw my advisor so I could discuss my strategy for next semester: lighter class load, no sciences. "I am coming up on a place in my life where I won't have the time available to excel in a demanding class the way I'd like," I lied, because I've been in that place since way before I even contemplated going back to school.

My advisor suggested I take Cultural Geography to fill a requirement.

"It won't bore me, will it?" I asked him. "Because some of my classes here have, and if I'm not engaged, I get surly and I sort of give up."

"By showing up and doing your work during the lecture, you will get an A," he said, which was his disguised way of confirming yes, it will bore me.

But I'm still looking forward to next semester, and the one after that. If the sad implosion of my performance in chemistry has taught me this much, what more thorny truths about myself could I discover? Class by class, I'll wrestle with demons more terrifying and impossible than those run-of-the-mill academic ones.

I thought that understanding the reason for your past failures made you impervious to future failures of the same sort, but here I am, wrong yet again. I've dreamed of going back in time, armed with the knowledge of my terminally ill bank account to come, so I could excel in high school and college instead of drifting through. But now I know that I'd make the same mistakes, only with more flair. Your problems don't go away, even when you acknowledge and accept them. They're still there to deal with, no matter how grown-up or deserving of success you feel you may be.

You can't just desire the result—in my case, the employment opportunities afforded by a fancy piece of paper with computer-generated calligraphy on it. You have to desire the *process*. There's no point in making bacon at home if you aren't enthralled with handling the meat, scrutinizing its progress as its flesh firms up in the dry cure, daydreaming of the savory lardons you will cut from it and fry up to top a salad of bitter greens. Making the bacon is the point; eating it is just the reward. I like learning about chemistry, but I love my family, and I can't click pause on this part of our lives together. Chemistry wants more of me than I can give it, now or maybe ever.

I doubt I'll go into nutrition. I'm much better at teaching people how to make pâté than I am telling them not to eat it. Wearing the costume of a future R.D. boosted my confidence a bit, but the outfit was ill-fitting. The only way I'll ever get any kind of degree will be slowly, leisurely, the way I prefer us to eat dinner. To earn an A in my chemistry class, I'd have to rely on frozen pizzas and skip the bedtime stories I look forward to reading to my daughter. My brain and my time and my kid are too valuable to squander on half-assing anything. Maybe I'll take chemistry twice. Not because I have to, but because I want to.

———
———

Observations Brought Back from the Zoo

By Marcia Aldrich

Nothing is simple. Nothing is pure. Sorrow folds inside the wings of happiness. And, as Louise Bogan says, "At midnight tears run into your ears."

*　　*　　*

Late last April, when the fist of winter in Michigan was finally letting go, I sat in my tiny office and received the news that my essay "The Art of Being Born" had been selected for inclusion in *The Best American Essays*. I let out a little whooping sound that died quickly, and then I bounded into the hall looking for someone to tell. The hall was empty. I took big gulps of air and sighed. I even hit my chest to quiet its banging. Returning to my office, my euphoria began to trouble me. Didn't I remember how once before, when I was carried away with my own good fortune, I looked through the windows of my dining room and watched as my neighbor's hospital bed was wheeled out the front door? Roger had died that morning, the morning of my good news.

Nothing is simple, no one emotion comes without the accompaniment of another, the wolf inside the grandmother, the tears running into the ears.

*   *   *

And sure enough I lost my balance.

In those early moments when the trees were finally leafing out and the world seemed warm and green again, I had only happy thoughts. I marveled at how an essay I had written for my daughter, detailing the day of her birth would be making its way to a larger audience. And then something brought me to a halt just as that hospital bed bumping down the front steps of the Gifford's house had tutored me in the scale of human suffering.

*   *   *

The Saturday evening before Mother's Day, my daughter called, the Clare whose birth I wrote about in "The Art of Being Born."

"Could you put the speaker phone on," she asked, "so I can speak to you and Daddy?" As we moved into the bedroom I thought that she might be calling to tell us she was in love. She's at the age when it wouldn't be surprising news.

No, it was nothing like that. She called to tell us she had cancer. I don't remember what words she said. My head was pounding too loudly to absorb everything she said. She tried to soften the blow, put a positive spin on it. I remember she said, *If you have to have cancer, thyroid cancer is the kind to have.* She was having a routine physical, and the doctor thought she felt something unusual in the area where the thyroid resides. She didn't think it was anything, Clare said, but just to be sure, she told Clare to have a biopsy.

Clare joked with her friends that she had goiter, and she hadn't been in a rush to have the biopsy done. She had just gotten the results a few days ago and they were positive. She did not call us with the news right away, I noted. It had taken a day or two for her to compose herself. She and her doctor felt certain they had caught the cancer early and that the prognosis was good.

Of course, it wasn't that simple. Her doctor had shielded Clare from the more complicated scenario. And Clare, in turn, shielded us, minimizing her illness at every turn. A few days later, the specialist ordered more biopsies. The cancer wasn't contained to the thyroid; they hadn't caught it early, and the removal of the thyroid was no longer going to be enough because the cancer had spread into the lymph nodes in the neck. Now she was going to have to have a radical neck dissection.

*   *   *

Mother's Day was cold. As if the weather was in concert with my internal revolution, it snowed. A week before when the weather suggested spring, friends had invited my husband and me to ride our bikes to the Potter Park Zoo in Lansing. I wasn't in any mood to go to the zoo or ride my bike through the snow. I was in shock. We should have bailed on the outing, but we didn't. I'm not sure why. Unbelievably, we thought it would be easier to go than to cancel. Or maybe we were just frozen. We both felt an obligation to be as positive as Clare was being. I felt her presence in everything I did or didn't do, and I knew she would be upset if we cancelled.

We went to the zoo with our friends, but we were shaken. I hadn't been to the zoo in over a decade. Zoos have always been mixed affairs for me. On the one hand, it's the only way to come into contact with wild animals, to be in their presence for a few moments. On the other, I can't glory in them for long without thinking about their caged existence, how their world has been shrunk to the size of whatever exhibit that the zoo was able to construct. Each exhibit is accompanied by signage that narrates a sad fate. Almost all the stories are of loss —the word *endangered* comes up over and over, shocking tales of the disappearance of habitat, poaching, with only the slightest ray of hope that something can be done in time. *In time.*

The others had moved inside the reptile house. I stood outside the bars of the snow leopard exhibit remembering the last time I had stood there with my children. I wondered if the snow leopard high up on the rock ledge, whose great grey eyes could be seen despite the camouflage by trees and shrubs and dusting of snow, was the same leopard I had seen before, or had that leopard died? I learned Serena is the current resident, born in captivity and fourteen years old, which would make it probable that she was the same snow leopard I remembered. Famously reclusive animals, they don't come down to preen close to the front of the exhibit where we would be able to see the deep grey and black rosettes on her body and the smaller spots on her head clearly. They hold themselves apart and, as in Yeats's epitaph, cast a cold eye "on life, on death."

A child several feet away said to his mother, *the animals don't look happy*. And it was true. The Amur tigers in the next exhibit—what was supposed to pass as a range– paced in agitated circles, never settling down. When they looked in my direction, they looked angry, waiting for something that would never come. Just then the snow leopard rose up onto her wide paws, flicked her enormously long tail and leapt from her ledge across the open space to another rock where she landed softly as she must have thousands of times in her fourteen years of captivity.

* * *

Shaken, shaken, shaken, that's what I was. The cold eye of the snow leopard, practiced in a kind of dying every day, was beyond me. There's nothing like thinking your child is safe and finding she is not and knowing nothing you can do will help. Everyone says this. I will hear it many times in the months to come and it will be true each time. Terrible things happen and we are daily surrounded by the news of them, but this wasn't a terrible thing happening to someone else—it was happening to my child, the child I had carried inside me and given birth to and held on my chest, the child who had changed my life in every conceivable way, who had made me jump across the abyss and love her.

I had spent much of my early adulthood steadfastly believing I didn't want children. I had doubts about my fitness as a mother born primarily from having been raised by a mother whose troubles had shaped my life. But as I started to turn away from the damage of my early life, I wanted to make the journey from young woman to mother, a journey, it turns out, that never ends, and decided to risk the free fall of childbirth.

In the last moments of my labor with Clare, she went into distress and I was wheeled into surgery. Despite pleas to stop pushing, I couldn't and as she crowned my midwife could see what was causing the distress—the umbilical cord had wrapped around Clare's neck. Each time I pushed, the cord tightened, cutting off her air. The mother knot, child and mother tied together, the essential couple. The midwife's quick hands undid the cord and set Clare free. For a moment, though, things were complicated, one thing attached to another, life attached to death, nothing simple, nothing pure, one thing turned into another in a blink of an eye. And though that first cord was cut, Clare and I are not severed. There is nothing that undoes me from her even as life undoes itself. Perhaps it would be better to be as practiced in resignation as the snow leopard perched on her allotted rock and not like the tigers that wait for what might never come, but I can't. I won't.

———
———

Contributors

MARCIA ALDRICH is the author of the free memoir *Girl Rearing*, published by W.W. Norton and part of the Barnes and Noble Discover New Writers Series. She has been the editor of *Fourth Genre: Explorations in Nonfiction*. *Companion to An Untold Story* won the AWP Award in Creative Nonfiction. She is at work on *Haze*, a narrative of marriage and divorce during her college years. Her website is MarciaAldrich.com.

SHAUN STALLINGS ANZALDUA is a writer, part owner of a country western nightclub, and a single mother of three teenagers. She and her kids live in Houston, Texas. She has a Master of Science in Agricultural Economics from the University of California at Davis. Her essays have appeared in *Brain, Child* and Full Grown People.

SARA BIR is a chef and food librarian. Her writing has appeared in *The Oregonian*, *Saveur*, *Section M*, and The Huffington Post. She's the former staff writer for the *North Bay Bohemian*, where her pop music criticism earned two AAN awards. Sara's also worked at a chocolate factory and a sausage cart, where she did not win any awards. Read her food writing at her blog, www.sausagetarian.com.

WILLIAM BRADLEY's work has appeared in a number of magazines and journals including Brevity, *Creative Nonfiction*, *The Bellevue Literary Review*, and *The Missouri Review*. He writes a column about pop culture for *The Normal School* and a column about creative nonfiction for *Utne Reader*. He has a wife, two cats, and all of the *Nightmare on Elm Street* movies on DVD.

SARAH WERTHAN BUTTENWIESER's essays have recently appeared in the *New York Times*, Salon, and the anthology *The Good Mother Myth* (Seal Press). Her articles have recently been published in *American Craft*, *Ceramics Monthly*, and *Edible Pioneer Valley* A regular contributor to Full Grown People, she makes her home in Western Massachusetts, with her husband and four children.

MICHELE COPPOLA is a Portland, Oregon, radio personality and copywriter whose work has been featured in *The Oregonian* and *Spot Magazine*, the literary journals *So To Speak* and *Short Story America*, and thousands of advertisements for overstocked car dealerships, furniture store liquidations, and monster truck shows. When she's not working, Michele volunteers with several animal welfare organizations and competes for couch space with her three dogs and husband Bryon. Ginger passed away two years ago in Bryon's lap and is still greatly missed.

Cover photographer **GINA EASLEY**'s favorite subjects to photograph are animals, children, nature, and all things beautiful and extraordinary. She is currently working on a series titled "Kindred Spirits," portraits of animals and their longtime human companions. Her work can be seen at www.ginaeasley.com and also at www.facebook.com/KindredSpiritsPhotoProject. Gina lives in Minneapolis.

ZAHIE EL KOURI writes about infertility, family, and multicultural America. Her work has appeared in *Mizna, a Journal of Arab American writing*, *Dinarzad's Children: an Anthology of Arab-American literature*, *Ars Medica: A Journal of Medicine, the Arts, and Humanities*, *Memoir Journal*, and *Brain, Child: The Magazine for Thinking Mothers*. She has an MFA from New School University, and has taught legal writing and fiction writing at the University of Oregon, the University of North Florida, Florida Coastal School of Law, Santa Clara University, and Stanford University. You can read more about Zahie and her writing at www.zahieelkouri.com.

JESSICA HANDLER is the author of *Braving the Fire: A Guide to Writing About Grief* (St. Martins Press, December 2013.) Her first book, *Invisible Sisters: A Memoir* (Public Affairs, 2009) is one of the "Twenty Five Books All Georgians Should Read." Her nonfiction has appeared on NPR, in *Tin House*, *Drunken Boat*, Brevity, *Newsweek*, *The Washington Post*, Full Grown People, and *More Magazine*. Honors include residencies at the Josef and Anni Albers Foundation, a 2010 Emerging Writer Fellowship from The Writers Center, the 2009 Peter Taylor Nonfiction Fellowship, and special mention for a 2008 Pushcart Prize. Featured as one of nine contemporary Southern women writers in Vanity Fair magazine, she learned to never again wear couture. Her website is www.jessicahandler.com.

KARRIE HIGGINS lives in Salt Lake City, Utah. Her writing has appeared in *Los Angeles Review*, *Quarter After Eight*, DIAGRAM, Mapping SLC, *Western Humanities Review*, *Black Clock*, and Full Grown People. Her essay, "The Bottle City of God," won the Schiff Award for Prose from the *Cincinnati Review*. She is at work on a book titled *Superman is my Temple Recommend*.

SONYA HUBER is the author of two books of creative nonfiction, *Opa Nobody* (2008) and *Cover Me: A Health Insurance Memoir* (2010), and a textbook, *The Backwards Research Guide for Writers* (2011). She teaches at Fairfield University and in Fairfield's low-residency MFA Program.

JENNIFER JAMES lives with her husband and three children in rural Virginia. After graduating from William and Mary in 1989, Jennifer moved to Gloucester County, where she found work as a teacher's assistant and veterinary receptionist until 2000, when her first child was born. After an approximate decade of diapers and interrupted sleep patterns, Jennifer started writing with purpose in 2010 and has been at it since. A good story is her favorite thing.

KIM KANKIEWICZ is an arts and culture writer and communications provider for businesses and nonprofit organizations. In addition to Full Grown People, her essays and articles have appeared in *Brain, Child*, *Pacific Standard*, Belt Magazine, the Minneapolis *Star-Tribune*, and elsewhere. She teaches writing to students of all ages and is the co-founder of a community-based literary arts organization called Eastside Writes. Kim lives in the Seattle area with her husband and children and a recalcitrant novel in progress.

KRISTIN KOVACIC teaches writing at the Pittsburgh High School for the Creative and Performing Arts and at Carlow University. For her essays, she has been awarded the Pushcart Prize and fellowships from the Pennsylvania Council on the Arts. She is the editor, with Lynne Barrett, of *Birth: A Literary Companion* (University of Iowa Press).

MEREDITH FEIN LICHTENBERG lives in New York City, where she is a Board Certified Lactation Consultant in private practice. Her writing has appeared in Full Grown People, *Brain, Child*, *The Mom Egg*, Tho Huffington Post, and elsewhere, and she can be found online at www.amotherisborn.com.

JODY MACE lives in Charlotte, North Carolina, where she publishes the website www.CharlotteOnTheCheap.com. Besides personal essays, which have appeared in *O Magazine*, *Family Fun*, *Wondertime*, *The Washington Post*, and many other publications and anthologies, she likes writing about music, travel, and local goings-on. She's always been a writer, but she spent some of her professional life as a computer programmer, shoe salesperson, musical transcriptionist, school librarian, and amusement park groundskeeper. She likes writing better. You can see more of her work at www.jodymace.com.

JON MAGIDSOHN is originally from Toronto, Canada. He's been featured in *The Guardian*, *The Bangalore Mirror* and on Brevity, Chicago Literati, Mojave River Review, Full Grown People and currently publishes three blogs. He's also written about fatherhood for dadzclub.com, The Good Men Project, and *Today's Parent* magazine. He's been an actor, singer, waiter, upholsterer, sales representative, handyman, dad, and writer. He and his family live in London but at the time of this printing are in Bangalore, India, where Jon writes full time. His website is www.jonmagidsohn.com.

JENNIFER MAHER teaches in the Gender Studies Department of Indiana University, in Bloomington, Indiana, where she lives with her family. Her work has appeared in *Feminist Media Studies*, *Bitch: Feminist Response to Popular Culture*, and *Brain, Child*. She has been nominated for two Pushcart Prizes.

ANTONIA MALCHIK's essays have been published in *The Boston Globe*, *Brain, Child*, *The Walrus*, *Creative Nonfiction*, *The Jabberwock Review*, many other newspapers and literary journals, and she worked formerly as a journalist in Austria and Australia. She is currently writing *Against the Grain*, a memoir about the lost competence of her pioneer ancestors and carving her way out of motherhood-induced depression through woodworking. She can be reached through her website, www.antoniamalchik.com.

CATHERINE NEWMAN is the author of the books *Waiting for Birdy* and *Field Guide to Catastrophic Happiness* (forthcoming), as well as the blog benandbirdy.blogspot.com, where she writes about parenting her kids and feeding her family. She still has only the real vagina.

JENNIFER NIESSLEIN is the founder and editor of Full Grown People. She's been published all over the damned place.

RANDY OSBORNE writes in Atlanta. A teacher of fiction and creative nonfiction at Emory University, he's finishing a book of personal essays, and is represented by the Brandt & Hochman Agency in New York. More about him at www.randyosborne.com.

CAROL PAIK lives in New York City with her husband and two kids. Her writing has appeared in the journals *Brain, Child*, *Tin House*, *The Gettysburg Review*, *Fourth Genre*, and *Literal Latte*, among others; and the anthologies *The Best Plays from the Strawberry One-Act Festival, vol. 6*, and *Contemporary Writers of/on Creative Nonfiction, fifth ed*. More of her writing at www.carolpaik.com.

SARAH PAPE lives and writes in Chico, California. She teaches English and works as the Managing Editor of *Watershed Review* at Chico State. Her poetry and prose has recently been published in *The Collapsar*, *Pilgrimage*, *Prick of the Spindle*, *The Squaw Valley Review*, *The Superstition Review*, and *Hayden's Ferry Review*. She curates community literary programming through the 1078 Gallery and is a member of the Quion Collective, a local letterpress group. She is currently working on a full-length collection of poems and a memoir.

KATY READ, a reporter for the Minneapolis *Star Tribune*, has published essays and articles in Salon, *Brain, Child*, Brevity, *River Teeth*, *More*, *Working Mother*, *Real Simple*, *Minnesota Monthly*, and other places. She has been nominated twice for a Pushcart Prize and been honored in literary competitions including the Chautauqua Literary Journal Prize for Prose, the Literal Latte Essay Awards, the William Faulkner-William Wisdom Creative Writing Competition and the Mid-American Review Creative Nonfiction Competition. She won a 2013 grant from the Minnesota State Arts Board and is working on a book about the culture of motherhood. Her website is www.katyread.com.

ROBIN SCHOENTHALER is a Boston-based cancer doctor (radiation oncologist), mother of two teen boys, and essayist. She writes about the experience of being a cancer doc, about parenting, and about all the crazy things that happen in our wild and precious lives. She's been published in Full Grown People, *Brain, Child*, the *Boston Globe*, *More Magazine*, *Readers' Digest*, *Pulse Magazine*, the *Boston Globe Magazine*, and a bunch of obscure medical journals.

AMBER STEVENS is a pseudonym for a writer from the desert Southwest, where she lives with her husband and two children. She enjoys writing essays and short stories and is working on a novel.

DINA STRASSER is a language arts educator of many stripes. She has been published in the *New York Times*, The London Times Online, and Orion Online, and she runs an award-winning blog on education at theline.edublogs.org.

JILL TALBOT is the author of *Loaded: Women and Addiction* (Seal Press, 2007), the co-editor of *The Art of Friction: Where (Non) Fictions Come Together* (University of Texas, 2008), and the editor of *Metawritings: Toward a Theory of Nonfiction* (University of Iowa, 2012). Her essays has appeared in journals such as Brevity, DIAGRAM, *Ecotone*, The Paris Review Daily, *Passages North*, The Pinch, The Rumpus, and *Under the Sun*. She lives in New Mexico.

SUZANNE VAN ATTEN is a features editor and writing coach for *The Atlanta Journal-Constitution*, a creative writing instructor at Shocking Real Life Learning Center, and author of the travel guide *Moon Puerto Rico*. Her essays, one of which was nominated for a Pushcart Prize, have appeared in the *Gettysburg Review* and *The Chattahoochee Review*, among other publications.

REBECCA STETSON WERNER lives in Portland, Maine, with her husband and three children. Trained as a child psychologist, she writes about parenting, children's books, adventures in urban homesteading, and life in their very old home at treetoriver.com. In addition to Full Grown People, she is a contributor to *Taproot Magazine* and Grounded Magazine.

SUSAN REBECCA WHITE is the author of the critically acclaimed novels *A Place at the Table*, *A Soft Place to Land*, and *Bound South*. Her essays have been featured in *Tin House*, Salon, the Huffington Post, and *The Bitter Southerner*. Susan lives in Atlanta with her husband Sam Reid and their son Gus.

To read more FGP essays,
visit **www.FullGrownPeople.com**.
New essays appear each Tuesday and
Thursday, and they're always free.